Experience in the Novel

Experience in the Novel

 SELECTED PAPERS FROM THE

ENGLISH INSTITUTE · EDITED WITH A

FOREWORD BY *Roy Harvey Pearce*

Columbia University Press · NEW YORK

AND LONDON · 1968

 FOREWORD

MODERN CRITICISM has been notoriously uneasy with the novel. Indeed, out of this freely admitted sense of uneasiness there have come many of the successes of our novelistic criticism: pieces in which the critic is able to ascertain and define those qualities, particularly in the modern novel, which often seem to be a sign of its having been transformed into something crucially different from what it was in the eighteenth and nineteenth centuries. In this sense, as is only proper, criticism orders itself according to the nature of the literary objects which it would confront. Still, whatever its modern transformations, there are in the novel as a literary form certain qualities, calling forth certain modes of experience, which are still much as they were in earlier times. Essentially, as a good deal of recent exacting historical criticism has shown, it is a matter of the novel's being tied to the detailed, iterated quality of life being lived through day-to-day, of the wholly absorbing sense of being *in* history, *in* society, *in* culture—and of being able to get out only temporarily and, as it usually develops, at one's peril. The novel, according to a definition set by its particular origins and functions, is characterized by a powerful and demanding sense of contemporaneity, actual or imagined, or both. As a form, it mediates sociocultural immediacy. Life lived through in the novel consequently derives from a series of infinitely complicated transactions between the self and a society of other selves, all in a matrix of dense institutional structures; the reader's experience must also derive from a series of such transactions. Nothing stands still, or can be made to stand still. Yet all that is relevant is at least potentially present. "Muchness," as Henry James said, seems always about "to overwhelm." The novel bulks large, as large as or larger than the aspects of life it would render in its own special way—and so rendering, comprehend. Thus we now freely say of all literary forms that they create "worlds." But I think it most significant that we did not get into the habit of so saying until we perforce tried to comprehend the novel. For par excellence it is the novel that creates a "world," even as it is created directly out of a "world." The process of creation entailed becomes precisely the reader's, and critic's, experience of that "world."

The essays here collected all deal in one way or another with the nexus of novelistic creation and novelistic experience. They are drawn from two conferences held at the twenty-sixth session of the English Institute. Those by Mr. Elliott, Mr. Miller, Mr. Hart, and Mr. Trachtenberg were delivered at a conference on "Criticism in Renewal: The Novel"; the latter two were Institute Prize Essays. Those by Mr. Frye and Mr. Fielding were delivered at a conference on Charles Dickens.

The essays, different as they are, try to account for the special ways we are (or should be) directly involved in the novels we read, and the particular conditions of the involvement. They all might be said to take as their point of departure sentiments like those expressed in these well-known words (from *Notes on the Novel*) of Ortega y Gasset:

> Let us observe ourselves at the moment we finish reading a great novel. It seems to us as if we are emerging from an-

other existence, that we have escaped from a world out of communication with our authentic world. This lack of communication is shown by the fact that transition from one to another is imperceptible. An instant ago we found ourselves in Parma with Count Mosca, Clélia and Fabrice; we were living with them, immersed in their air, their space, their time [*tiempo*]. Now suddenly without any intermission we find ourselves in our chamber, in our city, in our date [*fecha*]; already our habitual preoccupations begin to awaken at the nerve ends. There is, of course, an interval of indecision, of uncertainty. Perhaps a brusque wing-stroke of memory will suddenly submerge us again in the universe of the novel and then with an effort as if struggling in a liquid element, we try to swim to the shore of our own existence. If someone should observe us then, he would see the dilation of eyelids which characterizes those who have been shipwrecked.[1]

Novelistic criticism might be described as an attempt to rescue the shipwrecked reader, in order to lead him to accept his present state as a necessary, if not sufficient, condition of his being altogether human.

ROY HARVEY PEARCE

University of California, San Diego
February, 1968

---

[1] The translation is Stephen Gilman's, done for his Institute essay, "The Novelist and His Readers: Meditations on a Stendhalian Metaphor," to be published by the Humanities Center of The Johns Hopkins University.

 CONTENTS

Experience in the Novel

George P. Elliott

THE PERSON OF THE MAKER

IF YOU WANT TO PRODUCE a complicated reaction in a storyteller, try telling him his fiction strikes you as being inevitable. He will of course be grateful to learn that his stories have hit you right, but, remembering all the false starts, wrong turnings, bungled opportunities, all the revisions, he knows how far from inevitable it was that this story was told in these and only these words. I have never heard of a novelist so Platonic that for him there was for *this* novel a preordained and perfect arrangement of words which it was his art to discover. It just doesn't feel like that to a writer when he is writing. So, you sophisticate your compliment; how beautifully he has created the illusion of inevitability. This will really bug him; for, if he was doing more than just amusing the reader, if he was trying to figure forth a truth, illusion was only a means to a substantial end. Terms such as necessity, organic unity, the inevitable form for the material can make even a novelist with Platonic views splutter: but but but. So you decide poets don't understand what they're saying any better now than they did when Socrates gave up on them.

I think we do, though, we writer-critics. There have been so many philosopher-critics and scholar-critics over the centuries, tidying up too much, getting things wrong here and there, explaining what can't be explained, that in mere defense we have said quite a lot about what we do, accumulated some wisdom on the matter, not enough to satisfy a Socratic probing, but some. Nor is there much chance that this dialogue between writer-critics and non-writer-critics will dry up. Tolstoy said of "a true work of art, that its content in its entirety can be expressed only by itself." [1] If this is true, as I take it to be, then so long as literature is being made there will be speculation on whether *that* material would have been better served by another shape than *this* one, and writers will continue to receive generous but inadequate praise which will evoke from them extensive, tricky, often impassioned, but sometimes less inadequate explanations.

A good many years ago I read a couple of novels by Ivy Compton-Burnett and was moved to do likewise. That is, I felt like writing a story in which the plot problem is announced at the outset, developed in clearly marked stages, and resolved at the very end, and in which all the characters are connected with the same family and speak concisely and hyperconsciously. I had no story or characters in mind, just the desire to play with this form. I was not concerned that my story might sound like a pastiche of Compton-Burnett. The world I lived in and knew well was the San Francisco Bay area in the mid-twentieth century. This raw material would oblige various modifications on the

---

[1] *Talks with Tolstoy* (1922), ed. A. B. Goldenveizer, trans. S. S. Koteliansky and Virginia Woolf (1923). As cited in Miriam Allott, *Novelists on the Novel* (New York, 1959), p. 235.

Compton-Burnett style if my story was to be at all credible—no large family mansions with servants; blurred, uncertain formalities within the family; different idiom and speech rhythms. For me to imitate her very closely would be to violate my experience. Besides, direct imitation would not have been as much fun as playing my game by some of her rules. The impulse to play by other people's rules obviously has a great deal to do with the game of parody, whether the parody is smooth, like Beerbohm's "The Mote in the Middle Distance," or rough, like Fielding's "Shamela." But it would not be surprising to learn that Dostoevsky got a similar impulse when he went to Dickens or Raymond Chandler when he went to Dashiell Hammett, and it would be even less surprising to learn that when Faulkner read Molly Bloom's soliloquy he thought "I want to do it too" and invented Benjy.

However the storyteller comes to make his initial formal choices, once they are made they will powerfully affect the material of the story. I based one of the characters in "A Family Matter" on myself; but what I chose to select and rearrange from my own personality conformed less to my knowledge of myself than to the requirements of that comic artifice, and the character is but a cousin to another one I based largely on myself in a novel, cousins twice removed. A far more substantial example of a consequence of formal choice is to be found in *Huckleberry Finn*.

Before he came to write that tale, Mark Twain had already invented the character of Huck, and I think it likely that, if he had chosen to tell this new tale in the third person, in the voice of adult indulgence which he used in *Tom Sawyer,* then

Huckleberry Finn would have been little more than its predecessor. To be at his best, Mark Twain had to get away from the respectable world into which he had married, in the guise of Samuel Clemens, and which he pleased for a living, which he dared displease only in private. To get away from respectability without displeasing it, this he could manage only at the double distance of speaking an idiom not his own and in a boy's voice. The choice to do this was, literarily, the most important Mark Twain ever made. Perhaps it was also the most fearful; at least, so one can speculate from the facts that he underestimated the book—he thought *The Personal Recollections of Joan of Arc* far better—and that the parts of *Huckleberry Finn* he liked to read aloud were the tamest, those which were most like *Tom Sawyer,* involving naughty-respectable Tom himself. Of course, writing in Huck's voice did not ensure excellence: *Tom Sawyer Abroad,* narrated by Huck, is poor stuff. All the same, it is displeasing to think of the Grangerford episode narrated in *Tom Sawyer* manner, and it is really painful to imagine Huck's temptation to betray Jim told that way. As it could have been: Mark Twain's decision to speak in Huck's voice looks a good deal more inevitable to us, I dare say, than it looked to him before he made it. In fact, he may not have decided at all; maybe he just fell into it.

I interrupted "A Family Matter" to write another story, "Children of Ruth," which originated not in a desire for formal play but in experience. I knew two upright, intelligent, strong, liberal women in Berkeley, both of whom had had serious difficulties with their children. Since I liked and admired them both,

I was troubled to understand what had gone wrong, and since my intellect jumbles when my emotions are strongly engaged, I would be able to understand these two women only if I wrote a story about a third woman somewhat like them, with children of my fostering. As for form, I took the one nearest to hand. That is to say, the story is formally conventional, traditional: here's a situation; first this happens, then that happens and means so and so, then something else meaning such and such; here's the outcome. I had only two special formal concerns, neither of them very important. The first was to make everything quite clear, so that I might understand the better and also because I was tired of hearing my friends complain that my fiction perplexed them; the second was to relieve the heavy, slow movement of the story by introducing midway a contrasting new element startlingly. But most of my attention went to working out what that woman and her children should do and say, not for the fun of it but for the understanding of it. The result is a longish story of considerably more force than comeliness, a kind of synoptic novel—a dwarf of a novel, head's all right but not enough body.

A good deal of fiction derives from the writer's impulse to understand or cause the reader to understand the true nature of part of the world. Whether he does it for himself primarily or for the readers he wants to affect does not matter as much as that he is pressed by the need to understand the world, to order experience. Often he is too pressed. Frank Norris, Theodore Dreiser, James Farrell, they did not play enough, and neither, like most autobiographical first novels, did *Stephen Hero*. If Harriet Beecher Stowe had slogged away naturalistically at her heavy job instead of playing in the manner of Scott and Dickens, *Uncle Tom's Cabin* would never have occasioned the comment, "So this is the little lady who made the big war." If Boswell had allowed himself to play with his material even more than he did, not only would Dr. Johnson be the greatest character in English literature but *The Life of Samuel Johnson* would be the greatest novel.[2]

Not long after writing these two stories I found myself arguing with a theologian who maintained that Aristotle was right, some people are natural slaves. Imagine: slavery not unjust? Since I can't think abstractly about anything as highly charged as this was for me at that time, I had to write a story. Of course I had heard the idea before, but it had had about as much meaning for me as phlogiston or Menippean satire, other people's vapors. However, shortly before arguing with my theological friend, I had met in Berkeley an American woman (black) who had been kept in slavery for twenty or more years by another American woman (white). At the time I knew her, the former slave was working, for wages, as a domestic servant for a gentle, civilized, liberal archeology professor and his psychoanalyst wife. The children of the slave's former mistress, now grown, had recently freed the slave by bringing suit against their mother and having her put in prison. By what underground route the former slave found herself working as a domestic for my friends, I forget. But it was clear to everyone that she was far happier than my friends about this legal, just relationship: they were barely able to behave like employers, but

[2] I owe this notion to Cecil Y. Lang.

she went on just like a slave out of Aristotle. "I shall serve you," she declared, and they said, "Please." Of course, I could have written a story based on that experience, a fantastic-seeming but actual story; and there were armed, well-trained, ready battalions of liberal emotions mutely demanding to be commanded forth by this real-life story. However, at the time, I had had a free and equal wife for several years, and a child with a will of her own. Aristotle's notion, illiberal and color-free, stayed in the forefront of my mind. In the apologue—or maybe it's a Menippean satire?—I wrote out of all this, "Sandra," I cut most of the ties to my own experience: the slave in the story is white, parents are off in the wings, slavery is imagined to be a twentieth-century American custom, and the narrator is a conventional young executive. The story is a playful meditation on authority and obedience.

Clearly a good many storytellers are failed philosophers whose intellectual ladders are not long and strong enough to get them out of the foul rag-and-bone shop of the heart. They may tell a parable as I did, or sprinkle their novels with essays as George Eliot did, or intellectify their characters like Mann in *The Magic Mountain.* They may attach the story to the idea with paste, like C. S. Lewis in *Perelandra,* or weld story and idea as Dickens did in *Bleak House,* vitalizing symbol, symbolizing life. No matter how, it is clear that the root and central stem of a lot of fiction is moral thought.

Idea, play, experience, these are important sources of fiction, though not the only ones. "Among the Dangs" was given me in a dream. I have produced a headless monster or two for money. Dickens was sometimes moved to effect social reform. Tolstoy in *Resurrection,* Richard Wright in *Native Son,* D. H. Lawrence sometimes, the Marquis de Sade always, they are out to convert their readers, and if William Burroughs is not intent on disordering his reader's mind I can't guess what he is up to. No doubt there are more sources yet—lust for fame, revenge, plain competitiveness. My point is that for a writer no story is inevitable but that to a reader an excellent story will feel inevitable. I think one must locate the source of this feeling of necessary order, not in any of the things I have mentioned thus far, but in that which finally unites them when they are united.

I take my texts from Tolstoy. "The most important thing in a work of art is that it should have a kind of focus, that is, there should be some place where all the rays meet or from which they issue. And this focus must not be able to be completely explained in words." [3] What makes a story more than a story? " . . . not the unity of persons and places, but that of the author's independent moral relation to the subject." [4] By putting these two passages together, one from Goldenveizer's *Talks with Tolstoy,* the other from Tolstoy's preface to a Russian translation of Maupassant, I mean to suggest a reciprocal relation between fictional materials, ideas, forms, on the one hand, and the person of the maker, on the other: they reach out toward and converge upon him; he reaches out toward and unites them with his moral vision. I have already been playing with some of the convergings; let me deal more seriously with moral vision, the ultimately important matter in making as well as in judging a

[3] Allott, *Novelists on the Novel,* p. 235.
[4] *Ibid.,* p. 131.

novel, that which the maker, while he is writing, can do little or nothing about since it is the essence of his person.

Fortunately, there exists a kind of paradigm upon which I can elaborate my argument. First there are Robbe-Grillet's novels and films, and his theoretical essays collected under the title *For a New Novel;* then there is a critical study of Robbe-Grillet by an American, Ben Stoltzfus, and now Stoltzfus's own "new novel" based on Robbe-Grillet's fictional methods. I argue from no special knowledge of either of these writers. I must confess that I have read only two of Robbe-Grillet's novels, *The Voyeur* and *Jealousy,* and have seen only one of his movies, *Last Year in Marienbad.* I shall speak primarily about *The Voyeur.*

The obvious question posed by this novel is: Did Mathias, the central character, rape and murder the girl (perhaps two girls?) or did he only fantasy the crime? Similar questions of fact are posed by *Jealousy* and *Marienbad,* as well, I understand, as by all Robbe-Grillet's other works. Some commentators treat the novels as puzzles and look for solutions. I throw in with those who think that it is part of the author's plan to raise such questions and leave them unanswerable. My primary reason for thinking he plans this is that the fiction is so very well put together. Here is a writer who knows what he is doing and does it expertly; if he leaves you asking what happened and who did it, surely he meant you to ask these questions, meant you to be unable to answer them. I find it an amusement—a tiny amusement, to be sure—to watch the puzzle-solvers take sides: Yes, Mathias killed her; No, he only fantasied it. For by the odd terms of this fiction, the ordinary question *Did he or didn't he?* changes character. Doubt about the facts of the story does not indicate an imperfection of plot but becomes, like the meticulous, objective description of the visual appearances of things, an essential part of the novel's strategy against the reader.

Moreover, we have the author's word in his essays. Of similar questions addressed to *Last Year in Marienbad,* he says in the essay "Time and Description": "Matters must be put clearly: such questions have no meaning. The universe in which the entire film occurs is, characteristically, that of a perpetual present which makes all recourse to memory impossible. This is a world without a past, a world which is self-sufficient at every moment and which obliterates itself as it proceeds. . . . There can be no reality outside the images we see, the words we hear." [5] Hume would have enjoyed this film, composed on his principles of cognition. Robbe-Grillet goes further: "Similarly, it was absurd to suppose that in the novel *Jealousy,* published two years earlier, there existed a clear and unambiguous order of events, one which was not that of the sentences of the book, as if I had diverted myself by mixing up a pre-established calendar the way one shuffles a deck of cards. The narrative was on the contrary made in such a way that any attempt to reconstruct an external chronology would lead, sooner or later, to a series of contradictions, hence to an impasse." [6] Now it is possible to assume, as

---

[5] Alain Robbe-Grillet, *For a New Novel: Essays on Fiction,* trans. Richard Howard (New York, 1965), p. 152. Acknowledgment is made to Grove Press for permission to quote from this work.

[6] *Ibid.,* p. 164.

Robert Martin Adams does,[7] that Robbe-Grillet's theoretical criticism is a lot of trickery, a big put-on: he contradicts himself, he applauds exegetes who contradict him, some of what he says is phenomenological nonsense. True. But I think that at least in "Time and Description" he is not kidding or horsing around. That is, what he says there about his fictional intentions is the best explanation I have seen; it jibes with what I think he is up to; even if he meant to be pulling the reader's leg there too, I will take this essay straight, for it states accurately what I take the intention of his work to be; his admirers warn us that he is shifty, but to be absolutely untrustworthy is to be in a sense trustworthy, and no one claims that for him. One does not need to trust the person of an essay-maker much to trust the essay's words: they are only conscious. Here is the last half of the paragraph I was just quoting on *Jealousy*. ". . . there existed for me no possible order outside that of the book. The latter was not a narrative mingled with a simple anecdote external to itself, but again the very unfolding of a story which had no other reality than that of the narrative, an occurrence which functioned nowhere else except in the mind of the invisible narrator, in other words of the writer, and of the reader."[8] Adams was right: Robbe-Grillet is a put-on artist. In the most literal sense, far more intimately than by flaying you and wearing your skin, he puts you on.

Ben Stoltzfus in his study *Alain Robbe-Grillet and the New*

[7] Robert Martin Adams, "Down Among the Phenomena," *Hudson Review*, Summer, 1967.

[8] *For a New Novel*, p. 164.

French Novel contradicts his master and asserts that Mathias in fact, not in fantasy, raped and killed one girl. "The plot, which revolves around the murder of the thirteen-year-old girl, Jacqueline, is not a tale told by an idiot, but visualized by a 'sex maniac.' The novel is full of 'violence sans objet' since the murderer, Mathias, has no 'reasonable' motive for his crime." [9] How can Stoltzfus be so sure? By importing the psychoanalytic technique of interpreting and applying it to selected cues (somewhat as Ernest Jones did to *Hamlet*). "We can say that Robbe-Grillet is initiating a new naturalism based on Freudian determinism." [10] So sure of this is Stoltzfus that in his own novel, *The Eye of the Needle,* published in 1967, he not only adapts Robbe-Grillet's fictional devices, which are admirable for suggesting a severely deranged consciousness; he also puts into practice the psychologizing he attributes to him. Here is a naked instance of literary influence: Stoltzfus read Robbe-Grillet, was moved by him, misunderstood him, then went and did somewhat likewise. At the outset of the novel, Stoltzfus's main character is unequivocally established as being insane; the story provides sufficient evidence for us to understand how the character was driven mad; all blurs, doubts, evasions, shifts, jumps in the story are attributable to his troubled mind and help us sympathize with him. In my view, Stoltzfus is wrong about Robbe-Grillet but correct about how to write good fiction: though there is a certain awkwardness in *The Eye of the Needle* which is not to be found in *The Voyeur* or *Jealousy,* it is a

[9] Ben Stoltzfus, *Alain Robbe-Grillet and the New French Novel* (Carbondale, Ill., 1964), p. 59.
[10] *Ibid.,* p. 64.

better novel than they, because of the author's moral vision.

I take psychoanalysis to be a variant of the Jewish-Christian ethical system. The arrogant dogmatism of the religious moralists is founded on their conviction that they have the revealed word of God to build on; the arrogant dogmatism of psychoanalytic moralists is founded on their conviction that they are not speculating on the contingent but building on scientific discoveries. But beneath their arrogancies, both are fundamentally concerned with the same nexus of motive, guilt, authority, love, responsibility. What are the rules of behavior, and how should they be modified? How keep from transgressing? How cure the ills of having transgressed? What are we like and how should we live? Because Stoltzfus is concerned with such matters, he distinguishes among his own person as maker, the person of his character, and you the reader, and this discrimination is not just literary in quality but also moral.

Robbe-Grillet, however, could not care less about such niceties of discrimination. He does not permit you to love, hate, or remain indifferent to Mathias, as you love, hate, or are indifferent to a person who is an other. You are to identify with Mathias, become him. Since Mathias is cut off from others, as disconnected as a man can be short of solipsism, catatonia, the padded cell, you are not permitted to connect with any of the other characters—not characters, named vacancies—in *The Voyeur*. Moreover, Robbe-Grillet is not an other for you to be connected with either. That novel imprisons you in a fearful, mad self. If, that is, you play its game. If you don't play its game but insist on otherness, on connections, if you straight-arm the author, you find yourself indifferent to all the named vacancies, including Mathias, but connected to Robbe-Grillet—by intense resentment at what he has tried to perpetrate on you. The one benefit I gained from reading *The Voyeur* was some notion of what a phenomenologist sees when he looks at the world. Case history. A document. Not a work of art.

I believe that there is no greater literary transgression than for the writer to put the reader on, that this is the ultimate possible fictional violation, and that Robbe-Grillet does it as well as it has been done. Stoltzfus, however, psychoanalytically moral through and through, says Robbe-Grillet puts the reader in the position of analyst. "His attack on psychological analysis in reality masks an intense fascination with the working of the mind, insomuch as his novels are the re-creation of a subjective world. It is the reader who, through the effect of his participation, is the analyst, and, by virtue of his insight into the projected images of things, sees and understands the mechanism of the protagonist's mind." [11] But that is not what Robbe-Grillet himself says. "Far from neglecting him, the author today proclaims his absolute need of the reader's cooperation, an active, conscious, *creative* assistance. What he asks of him is no longer to receive ready-made a world completed, full, closed upon itself, but on the contrary to participate in a creation, to invent in his turn the work—and the world—and thus to learn to invent his own life." [12] That is to say, he intends his fiction to supply you with materials, and a few guidelines, which you are to employ in making your own creations—of a novel (your *Jealousy,* not the *Jealousy*), of the world, of your self.

[11] *Ibid.,* p. 65.

[12] *For a New Novel,* p. 156.

Not even Joyce was that immodest. All he wanted was for you to spend *your* life reading *his* books. Robbe-Grillet wants you to become him. As writer and novel-maker, he becomes Mathias; as reader and novel-maker, you must become Mathias; both you and he become that same person, unholy three in one. According to the New Novelists, it is old-fashioned to reimagine a novel which the author imagined in the first place; since the New Novel exists only as it is becoming without having a defined form to become, since it is created each time the first time, the reader creates the novel just as the author did; the author's contribution, presumably, is to give the reader the materials and a few rules for making his own novel—a do-it-yourself kit. But you are not to create just the novel: you are also to create the world and your own self, since the world and the self also have to be created each moment afresh. The best term I can find for this attitude is a pretty, if flimsy, oxymoron, creative nihilism.

Robbe-Grillet is a sort of anti-guru, the Ignatius of nothingness. According to his instructions, to read one of his novels is to go into spiritual training for perpetual creating. Well, speaking for myself, thanks anyway but no, I'm too slothful to play the strenuous game of creative nihilism, and if I did feel like playing it I know better rules than Robbe-Grillet's to play it by. Or maybe he is out to get me to make up my own rules? Thanks again, but the answer is still no. I can't get it out of my head that the world was already here, equipped with rules of its own, when I was born into it, and as for that sad little sack of self I was born with, I guess maybe I've had a hand in shaping it up, but so did lots of other people and institutions and forces, many of which I don't so much as know to thank.

I have a friend, a subtle, honest, quick woman, herself a novelist, who is much drawn to the New Novel. Each of us, she says, goes about in the world unable to know the most important part of it, his own head, the space behind the eyes and between the ears where his self, the *I,* is located. The New Novel brings things to focus exactly on that space, saying in effect, "You can't know who you are; here is somebody to be." My friend was thinking primarily of *Jealousy* and of Nathalie Sarraute's *The Golden Fruits,* not of Robbe-Grillet's theoretical essays, which she had not read.

As I see it, this opinion renders meaninglessly arbitrary the fundamental human assertion "I am"—the "I am" in which is implied "you are" and after which comes "I am myself; you are yourself." I don't know how to go any further in than those assertions go. There are in fact people who cannot say "I am," and there are those who say "I am not anybody." Surely it is well to help them get back to the beginning "I am," and to aim them at "I am myself." Surely it is ill to do as Robbe-Grillet does, to get them to say "I am nobody" and then aim them at "I am somebody else." The religious teachers tell us that in order to become yourself you must lose yourself. But there are ways and ways of losing yourself. To do it by becoming simultaneously a rapist-murderer (or fantasist of rape-murder) and a put-on artist, surely there is a better way to lose yourself than that.

Let me quote Tolstoy again on the unifying principle in fiction: "the author's independent moral relation to the subject." And, I would add, his independent moral relation to the reader. One hardly goes to fiction for moral instruction in such matters as the evils of raping and murdering little girls. Fiction is an inextricably moral art not because of prepackaged admonitions and exempla but because of the complex, intimate relationship of author to subject-matter and of author to reader. Tolstoy said: "Whatever the artist depicts, whether it be saints or robbers, kings or lackeys, we seek and see only the soul of the artist himself." [13] Myself, I much like one of the ways Chekhov took. In "Ward Six" he in his own person invites me in my own person to go with him into the small wing of a dreadful provincial hospital. "If you are not afraid of being stung by the nettles, come with me along the narrow path leading to the annex, and let us see what is going on inside." [14] He introduces the keeper and the five madmen, and tells me what he thinks of them—of one especially. "I like his broad pale face with its high cheekbones, an unhappy face in which a soul tormented by perpetual struggle and fear is reflected as in a mirror. . . . I like the man himself." [15] Chekhov then retires and lets me get to know the doctor well, allows me—makes it possible for me—to follow the doctor's terrible descent into confusion and unredemptive loss of self and life. Because I do not confuse myself with the doctor, my pity for him does not mask pity for myself. Because I do not confuse myself with Chekhov, my enormous gratitude to him contains no self-congratulation. I did not create that story, he did. He made it and invited me in.

I am well aware of the objection to these views of mine: out of date, relativistic world, twentieth century, era of individual-

---

[13] Allott, *Novelists on the Novel,* p. 131.

[14] Anton Chekhov, *Ward Six and Other Stories,* trans. Ann Dunnigan (New York, 1965), p. 7.

[15] *Ibid.,* p. 9.

ism is over, humanism, we have changed all that, spirit of the age. Robbe-Grillet is a bit conventional—even respectable perhaps?—in bothering in his essays to belabor the stupidity of applying archaic, quaint, nineteenth-century moral standards to contemporary life and literature. For example, he permits himself the banality of observing that in the Balzacian novel "time played a role, and the chief one: it completed man, it was the agent and measurement of his fate." [16] But after this stumble he catches his balance and does what is only de rigueur for an up-to-date French intellectual in his position these days, he disposes of practically everything else. "In the modern narrative, time seems to be cut off from its temporality. It no longer passes. It no longer completes anything. . . . Here space destroys time, and time sabotages space. . . . Moment denies continuity." [17] I do not know what he means by all this, but I think he means it. It is a coherent extension into blatant inscrutability of his other less extreme opinions and practices.

I take this as being valuable chiefly as a symptom of the greatest modern intellectual idolatry, adoration of the *Zeitgeist*—not the *Geist* of our particular *Zeit,* but *Zeitgeist* as a god—not a good god but a powerful one, necessary to obey, to keep up with, not to fall behind, never never to deny or challenge. But this is not the occasion for taking on Hegel, and besides I lack the intellectual artillery to do the job right. So far as I can see, the Hegelian *Zeitgeist* operates as a sort of cosmic CIA with all halfway-conscious people in its pay whether they are knowingly spooks or not.[18] Well, Robbe-Grillet is a spook all

[16] *For a New Novel,* p. 154.

[17] *Ibid.,* p. 155.   [18] I owe this simile to R. V. Cassill.

right, but I don't think Chekhov was and I hope I am not. I don't see why you have to write evil stories just because the age is evil. There are other powers to be secret agents of.

I could—one could—find out a good deal about M. Alain Robbe-Grillet, the man in history, even meet him and talk with him; but when I read *The Voyeur* I have only a blurred, hollow sense of the person who made it. I know little of Lady Murasaki and nothing of the nameless Icelander who wrote *Njal's Saga;* but when I read either of them, I have a strong, clear sense, which I cannot define in words, of the person of the unknown maker.

J. Hillis Miller

THREE PROBLEMS OF FICTIONAL FORM:

FIRST-PERSON NARRATION IN *David Copperfield*

AND *Huckleberry Finn*

ANY WORK OF LITERATURE, including any novel, is the verbal expression of a consciousness. The words on the page give the reader access to another mind, its feelings and thoughts, its way of encountering an imagined world. Criticism of fiction, like the criticism of other forms of literature, begins with an act of reading which may be defined as consciousness of the consciousness of another. The critic must, as far as possible, dispossess himself of his own mental structures and attempt to coincide, in an act of pure identification, with the mental structures of the novel. Criticism is a putting in words of the results of this approach toward identification.

A novel, however, has special structures of its own. To these pertain the special problems of the criticism of fiction. As critics like Georg Lukács, Ortega y Gasset, Lionel Trilling, and Ian Watt have assumed,[1] the novel came into existence in a particu-

---

[1] See Georg Lukács, *Die Theorie des Romans* (Neuwied and Berlin, 1963; first published in 1914–15); José Ortega y Gasset, *The Dehumanization of Art and*

lar time in the history of Western man and therefore expresses
the personal, social, and metaphysical experiences of man during
that time. The rise of the novel is associated with a new discovery of the isolation and autonomy of the private mind, with
a sense of the absence of any preestablished harmony between
the mind and what is outside the mind, with a diminishing
faith in the existence of any supernatural power giving order
and meaning to this world, and with a turning to relations between persons as the chief, if not exclusive, source of authentic
life for the individual. The novel is the form of literature developed to explore the various forms intersubjective relations may
take. If reading a novel is consciousness of the consciousness of
another, the novel itself is a structure of related minds. To read
a novel is not to encounter a single mind but to take part in an
interaction among several minds—the relation of the narrator to
the protagonists, of the protagonists to one another. The narrator is one mind among others, and the question of point of
view or narrative stance may be assimilated into the question of
relations between minds. Intersubjectivity is an important dimension of fictional form, and a sensitive discrimination of the
ways minds are related to one another in a given novel is a primary requirement in the interpretation of fiction.

A second aspect of fictional form is time. Time is constitutive for the novel in a way which makes it different from other
forms of literature. Any work of literature has a temporal rather

---

Other Writings on Art and Culture (Garden City, N.Y., 1956); Lionel Trilling,
The Liberal Imagination: Essays on Literature and Society (New York, 1950),
and Beyond Culture: Essays on Literature and Learning (New York, 1965); Ian
Watt, The Rise of the Novel: Studies in Defoe, Richardson, and Fielding (Berkeley and Los Angeles, 1957).

than a spatial form. It takes time to read it. The words follow one another in time and establish in their sequence a temporal rhythm of connections and relationships. In a short lyric poem, however, the beginning and ending are so close to one another that they appear to be virtually simultaneous. This generates the illusion of spatial form and gives rise to a whole critical vocabulary of spatial terms: "pattern of imagery," "ironic juxtaposition," "design of the whole," and so on. Moreover, our language and our imaginations are strongly spatialized, rich in spatial terms and poor in temporal terms. It is much easier to talk about a work of literature as if it were a spatial mosaic than to do justice in critical language to its temporality. Nevertheless, the fundamental dimension of literature is time.

This becomes especially important in a work of literature as long as a novel. A simultaneous possession by the reader of all the words and images of *Middlemarch, À la recherche du temps perdu,* or *Ulysses* may be posited as an ideal, but such an ideal manifestly cannot be realized. It is impossible to hold so many details in the mind at once. To point to the fact that all the words do exist side by side on the page and the pages side by side in the book is to commit the error of thinking of the work of literature as a physical object, like a stone or a tree, rather than as a structure of signs.[2] The novel exists, it is true, as black marks on the pages, but it exists as a work of literature only as it is read. As such, it is not a spatial structure of simultaneously related parts but an ever-changing rhythm of relationships. The

[2] See Paul de Man, "New criticism et nouvelle critique," *Preuves,* No. 188 (October, 1966), pp. 30–34, for a discussion of this distinction in terms of the concept of intentionality.

passage being read at a given time constitutes itself as the
momentary center of the work. The rest of the novel organizes
itself with varying degrees of immediacy around that temporary
center.

To think of a novel in this way is to confront what might
be called the paradox of the first and second reading. Which is
the proper reading of a novel, the first reading, when the outcome of the story is in doubt for the reader, so that he is experiencing the events as if they had an open future, like his own life
as he lives it, or the second reading, when the future is known
from the beginning and the full significance of all the passages
understood as they are encountered? To meet this paradox is to
glimpse the hidden connections among the several problems of
fictional form. In most novels, as a matter of fact, the reader is
put even in the first reading virtually in possession of the perspective allowed by the second reading, that perspective which
no one in "reality" can have on himself while his life continues.
The protagonists live their lives in ignorance of the future. The
narrator speaks from the perspective of the end. The reader
enjoys both these points of view at once. He experiences the
novel as the reaching out of the protagonists' point of view
toward the narrator's point of view, as if they might at some
vanishing point coincide. This reaching out toward complete-
ness, in which the circle of time will be drawn closed, is the
essence of human temporality. It may therefore be said that a
novel as it is read from passage to passage, brought into existence as a structure of meanings, expresses a distinctive form of
lived human time.

The importance of human time as the constitutive dimension for the novel may be approached from another direction. Premodern forms of narrative literature, for example, the epic, were often structured around the relationship between human time and divine or eternal time. Many critics, notably Ortega y Gasset and Georg Lukács, have centered on a comparison with the epic their attempts to define the unique qualities of the novel. One difference between the epic and the novel is a difference in the kinds of time expressed in each. On the one hand, there is the mythical time of the epic, with its eternal repetition of celestial archetypes. These put human time in relation to the end of time or to an escape from time. Christian epics like *The Divine Comedy* or *Paradise Lost* are based on allegorical or anagogical conceptions of time which again put human time in close relationship to God's time. Human time, in Christian literature, is a moving image of eternity. The novel, however, tends to be a post-Christian form of literature, a form which assumes that God is distant or dead. In such a form the connection between human time and divine time is broken. Man's time is experienced as determined by its finitude. It becomes the dimension in which man experiences his lack of fullness of being, the impossibility of a permanent attainment of an ideal life. Though Lukács remains bound within a linear conception of human time,[3] he has nevertheless provided in *The Theory of the Novel* a striking formulation of the way time is essential to modern fiction:

> Time then can first become constitutive when the connection with the transcendent homeland is broken. . . . It is

[3] See Paul de Man, "Georg Lukács's *Theory of the Novel*," *Modern Language Notes*, LXXXI, No. 5 (December, 1966), 533–34.

only in the novel, the content of which consists in a necessary quest for essence and in an inability to find it, that time
is an inseparable part of the form . . . . In the epic, the
immanence of meaning within life is strong enough to abol-
ish time.[4] Life as such accedes to eternity . . . . In the novel,
meaning and life separate and, with them, essence and time;
one could almost say that the whole inner action of the
novel is no more than a struggle against the power of time.[5]

If temporality is constitutive in new ways for the novel, so
are there new structures in the relation of imaginary and real.
The question of realism is a third problem of fictional form.
Traditional theories of fictional realism are based on a representational dualism, often expressed in the image of a mirror, as in
Stendhal's often-cited description of a novel as "un miroir qu'on
promène le long d'un chemin." On one side there is reality, the
solid substance of the social and physical world. On the other
side there is the novel, which must mirror this reality as exactly
as possible in words. George Eliot, in the seventeenth chapter of
Adam Bede (1859), provides one of the best expressions of this
mimetic theory of realism. "[M]y strongest effort," she says,

---

[4] Lukács refers here to transcendent meaning, supernatural meaning.

[5] Lukács, *Theorie,* pp. 125–26: "Die Zeit kann erst dann konstitutiv werden,
wenn die Verbundenheit mit der transzendentalen Heimat aufgehört hat. . . .
Nur im Roman, dessen Stoff das Suchen-müssen und das Nicht-finden-Können
des Wesens ausmacht, ist die Zeit mit der Form mitgesetzt . . . . In der Epopöe
ist die Lebensimmanenz des Sinnes so stark, dass die Zeit von ihr aufgehoben
wird: das Leben zieht als Leben in die Ewigkeit ein . . . . Im Roman trennen
sich Sinn und Leben und damit das Wesenhafte und Zeitliche; man kann fast
sagen: die ganze innere Handlung des Romans ist nichts als ein Kampf gegen
die Macht der Zeit."

"is . . . to give a faithful account of men and things as they have mirrored themselves in my mind. The mirror is doubtless defective; the outlines will sometimes be disturbed, the reflection faint or confused; but I feel as much bound to tell you as precisely as I can what that reflection is, as if I were in the witness-box narrating my experience on oath." [6]

The connection of the question of realism with the question of intersubjectivity appears clearly in this text. The reflections in the mirror are not, in George Eliot's formulation, initially the words and images of the novel. They are the duplication in the mind of the beholding artist of "men and things" in the outside world. The novel springs from the response of the mind of the novelist to the minds of others as they are embodied in appearances. The novel itself is a representation of this representation, an "account" of it in words, the copy of a copy.

Georges Blin, in the introduction to *Stendhal et les problèmes du roman*,[7] has shown in masterly fashion the contradictions and paradoxes of this traditional theory of realism, and many recent critics have turned their attention to elements of the "anti-novel" present even in works of fiction addressed most unambiguously to the work of representational realism. One of these contradictions is brought into the open in the passage from *Adam Bede*. A novel is an objective imitation, a cunning model in words of a reality to which it should, like a photograph, correspond point for point. At the same time it is the account of someone's experience of reality. It has a mental, not a physical,

[6] *Adam Bede*, in *Works*, Cabinet Edition (Edinburgh and London [1877–80]), I, 265–66.

[7] (Paris, 1960), pp. 5–16.

existence, therefore is unable to escape the necessary defects, disturbances, indistinctions, and confusions of any subjective mirroring of reality.

More important still is the paradoxical fact that a novel is based on reality, impossible without it, constantly referring to it whether accurately or with subjective distortions, and at the same time is an autonomous structure of words creating its own independent reality, a world which may be encountered nowhere but in the pages of this particular book. The anti-novelistic elements which creep into the most unequivocally mimetic fiction are those details in the language in which the novel turns back on itself. This reflexive movement reveals the fact that the novel is not the report of a witness of actual events, but something made up by its author, a lie, a fiction, the generator of its own reality rather than the reflection of a reality outside itself. An example of this is the contrast between those passages in Scott's novels, often given as footnotes, in which he calls attention to the historical accuracy of some event or of some detail of dress or custom, and those passages in which he asserts the fictive nature of his narrative, the fact that he has made the story up out of his imagination.

The structure of this conflict between the imaginary and the real is intrinsic to the novel. It perhaps finds its origin in the fading of faith in celestial models or archetypes which would give a narrative stability and ground it in the transcendently real. Such a supernatural ground would be the source and sanction both for works of art and for the objective world, that artwork of God's. In place of this secure structure of correspond-

ences, the novel often puts an overlapping or interaction of real
and imaginary which is like those optical illusions which may
be seen as right-side-up or upside-down, inside-out or outside-in,
depending on how they are looked at, and come, as one looks, to
vibrate with dizzying rapidity between the first orientation and
the second.

This alternation of true and false is easiest to see in the
interpenetration of minds (and therefore of levels of reality)
which makes up a novel. The narrator of a novel may sometimes seem to be the novelist himself, speaking in his own voice,
as in many passages in *Tom Jones* (1749), or in *Vanity Fair*
(1847–48), or as in those notorious interventions in Trollope's
novels which Henry James deplored. At other times the narrator
may exist entirely on the other side of the mirror. In this case he
is a persona or invented voice of the author who speaks as if the
events he retells had an historical existence. The narrative voice
in many novels goes back and forth without warning from one
side of the mirror to the other.

Another place to see this vibration is in the use of stories
within stories, or narrators within narrators. These have been
part of fictional technique from the Renaissance to the present
and may be traced from the puppet-show of Master Pedro and
the interpolated stories in *Don Quixote* (1605; 1615), through
the interpolated stories and use of scenes in the theater in Fielding's novels to nineteenth-century works like *Pickwick Papers*
(1836–37), *Wuthering Heights* (1847), *Bleak House* (1852–
53), and *The Moonstone* (1868), and on to the complex use of
multiple narrators by Conrad and others in the twentieth cen-

tury. The effect of these reflections within reflections is curious. It parallels the effect of the play within the play in Renaissance drama.[8] The palpably fictive or subjective quality of the interpolated story tends to affirm the historical reality of the first level of the narration, but at the same time the reader may be led to see that he is himself hearing a story, like the characters on the first level of reality in the novel. The reader may then come to feel like the first participant in an echoing series of representations within representations, each equally real and equally imaginary, each affirming the reality of the preceding one and yet at the same time undermining it, like the endless sequence of images when two mirrors are held up to reflect one another's reflections. All the world's a novel, and the men and women merely characters in it, creating and sustaining their own illusory universes.

Intersubjectivity, time, and realism—each of these aspects of fiction has the same form. Each leads to the others and reveals its congruity with them. Each is so entangled with the others that it cannot be detached and investigated in isolation. All three have the form of an incomplete circle, a circle in which consciousness moves away from itself in order to move back to its ground.

Moving toward itself by moving away from itself, however, the mind never reaches its goal. Though human temporality is a reaching from the present toward the future to reappropriate the past, the circle of time is never complete. Past and future never

---

[8] See S. L. Bethell's discussion of this in *Shakespeare and the Popular Dramatic Tradition* (Durham, N.C., 1944), p. 39.

come together in the present. Though art may be defined as a search for the real by way of the imaginary, the echoing sequence of reflections is never stilled in a coincidence of the fictive and the true. Though interpersonal relations may be defined as a search for the true self by way of other people, a man never fully possesses his buried self by means of his possession of another person.

To move toward these goals, nevertheless, is a momentary revelation of them, as well as a failure to reach them. As long as the fiction continues it holds in the open the incomplete structure of temporality, of the imaginary seeking to become the real, and of one mind trying to reach its hidden depths through others. Holding this never-finished structure in the open, the novel also holds in the open a glimpse of its ground, its secret origin and end.

When the fiction is over the revelation is over, over in open-ended fiction in the silence after the last page of a failure of the protagonist to coincide wholly with the narrator, over in closed forms of fiction in the disappearance of the protagonist's detached self-consciousness when he finds his true self and dissolves into the collective consciousness of the community. American novelists have tended to feel that authenticity lies in maintaining one's separate individuality. In English fiction, even in the twentieth century, the attainment of a proper self has often seemed to coincide with the discovery of a place in the community. For such novelists the goal for the individual is the assimilation of his private mind into that public mind for which the omniscient narrator is a spokesman.

David Copperfield (1849–50) and *Huckleberry Finn* (1884), among nineteenth-century English and American novels, are salient examples of masterworks of fiction written as first-person narratives. The first-person novel, in spite of Henry James's distaste for its baggy looseness, is not so much formless as a special case of fictional form. It provides a good example of the interaction of the three aspects of that form.

The distinguishing characteristic of the first-person novel is the fact that the narrator in most cases coincides with the protagonist. This does not mean, however, that in this coincidence the structure of intersubjective relations usual in the third-person novel is truncated or collapsed. Rather, it takes another form. In *David Copperfield* or *Huckleberry Finn* the author attempts to come to terms with his own life by playing the role of an imaginary character who in both cases has obvious similarities to the author himself. This imaginary character, in his turn, retraces from the point of view of a later time the earlier course of his life. The interpersonal texture of both novels is made up of the superimposition of two minds, the mind of the adult David reliving his experiences as a child, the mind of Huck after his adventures are over retelling them from the perspective of the wisdom, if wisdom it is, to which they have led. In both novels the older narrator, from the vantage of a later time, watches his younger self engage himself more or less naively in relations to other people. Behind this double consciousness may be glimpsed the mind of the author himself, the Charles Dickens who is reshaping the events of his life to make a novel out of them, the Mark Twain who is present in the irony which runs through *Huckleberry Finn* as a pervasive stylistic flavoring. This stylistic quality results from Huck's inability to understand his experiences, either while they are happening or as he retells them, as well as the reader and the author understand them.[9] From author to narrator to youthful protagonist to other characters—the structure of *David Copperfield* or *Huckleberry Finn* is no less than that of *Pride and Prejudice* (1813), *Middlemarch* (1871–72), or *The Golden Bowl* (1904), a pattern of related minds. In both first-person novels the author may be seen going away from himself into an imagined person living in an imagined world in order to return to himself and take possession by indirection of his own past self and his own past life.

If intersubjective relations and relations of the imaginary and the real are so closely intertwined in these two first-person novels, they both provide classic examples of the incomplete circle or spiral form taken by temporality in fiction. The autobiographical novel has exactly the structure of human temporality. It is a moving toward the future in order to come back to what one has already been, in an attempt to complete one's deepest possibility of being by drawing the circle of time closed and thereby becoming a whole. But the circle of time is complete only with my death. As long as I live I cannot reach that future moment when I shall understand myself completely, coincide completely with the hidden sources of my being. Going

[9] Examples of this are Huck's discussions of the efficacy of prayer: "[T]here's something in it when a body like the widow or the parson prays, but it don't work for me, and I reckon it don't work for only just the right kind," or the episode in which Huck, having been roundly defeated by the subtle enthymemes of Jim's rhetoric, says: "I see it warn't no use wasting words—you can't learn a nigger to argue. So I quit" (*Adventures of Huckleberry Finn,* ed. Sculley Bradley, Richmond Croom Beatty, and E. Hudson Long, Norton Critical Edition [New York, 1962], pp. 34, 67; further references to this novel will be by page numbers in this edition).

forward in time through a recapitulation in language of his experiences in the past, the narrator of a first-person novel returns
eventually back through his past to himself in the present, but at
a higher level of comprehension, it may be, than he had when
he began to tell his story. The insight born of the act of retelling
may lead the narrator to an authentic understanding of his life,
a recognition of its hitherto hidden patterns. On the basis of this
recognition he may then take hold of his past life, accept it in a
new way in the present, and come to a resolute decision about
the future. This revelation, however, is never complete as long as
the narrator lives. The spiral is endless. Huck or David could go
around and around the circle indefinitely, bringing their past
lives up to the present in the light of the new insight gained by
the act of retelling, recapitulating their lives over and over without exhausting them or finding that a new circling repetition
had brought them back to exactly the same place.

Even so, the moment of return from a journey through the
past to the present, when the two levels of the narrator's mind
coincide, is the crucial instant in a first-person novel. It is the
moment at the end of *Huckleberry Finn,* for example, when
Huck speaks in the present tense of his present situation. Having gone through his life up to the present, he sees it whole and
sums up what he sees in his decision to run away from civilization. Only in this way can he escape from another repetition of
his repetitive adventures, adventures which have rhythmically
alternated between solitude and disastrous involvement in society, and are about to culminate, as Daniel Hoffman and others
have seen,[10] in a recurrence of the involvement most dangerous

[10] See Daniel G. Hoffman, *Form and Fable in American Fiction* (New York,
1961), p. 342.

of all to his integrity: subjection to the loving-kindness of a well-meaning member of respectable society. "But I reckon I got to light out for the Territory ahead of the rest," says Huck, "because Aunt Sally she's going to adopt me and sivilize me and I can't stand it. I been there before" (226).[11]

At the end of *David Copperfield* David, like Huck, returns after a long looping circuit through his past to present-tense speech about the present. He too looks toward the future on the basis of a clear understanding of the past and makes a decision about that future. But how different is his state of mind! How different is his relation to other people, and how different the resolution he takes! David has experienced in childhood, like other Dickensian heroes or heroines, Oliver, Pip, Arthur Clennam, or Esther Summerson, solitude and deprivation, the lack of a satisfactory place within a family or within society. He has been "a somebody too many"[12] "cast away among creatures with whom [he has] had no community of nature" (105). His search through the adventures he retells is for something which will focus his life and give it substance. Throughout his experiences he is troubled by "a vague unhappy loss or want of something" (386). He seeks something to fill the void in his heart. The novel is his "written memory" (527), in which the adult David, as he says, "stand[s] aside, to see the phantoms of those

---

11 See Roy Harvey Pearce, " 'The End. Yours Truly, Huck Finn': Postscript," *Modern Language Quarterly,* XXIV, No. 3 (September, 1963), 253–56, for a discussion of the ironic historical actualities behind Huck's reference to the "Territory." The Territory is the Indian Territory, which was to become Oklahoma, and Huck's solitude if he were to go there would soon be invaded by the same "civilizing" people he has encountered along the Mississippi.

12 *David Copperfield,* ed. George H. Ford, Riverside Edition (Boston, 1958), p. 99. Further references will be to page numbers in this edition, which reprints the Charles Dickens Edition of 1868–70, the last to be revised by the author.

days go by me, accompanying the shadow of myself, in dim procession" (479). *David Copperfield,* like Thackeray's *Henry Esmond* (1852), contains many references to time and memory. These call the reader's attention to the distance between the present condition of the narrator and that of his past self. They interpose between the one and the other "a softened glory of the Past, which nothing could [throw] upon the present time" (494). Retracing the journey which has led him step by step to the present, David seeks to find the source of the cohesive force which associates each detail with the others and gradually organizes them all, as he retells them, into the pattern which constitutes his destiny.

Is it a private power of feeling in David which does this, a subjective energy of association? The many references to the psychology of association suggest that this is the case. Agnes is "associated" in David's mind with "a stained glass window in a church" (176), just as the image of Ham's anguish after little Em'ly runs away "remain[s]," says David, "associated with that lonely waste, in my remembrance, to this hour" (347), or as David says of Steerforth's death: "I have an association between it and a stormy wind, or the lightest mention of a sea-shore, as strong as any of which my mind is conscious" (599). It may be such associations which gather all the events of David's life together and make them one.[13]

---

[13] David's profession, which grows from the qualities which give him his power of fanciful association, reinforces this theme. His writing of fiction constitutes a realm of the imaginary within the imaginary. Dickens writes a novel about someone who writes novels. On this side of the mirror *David Copperfield* is a work by Dickens which transposes his life into a fiction. On the other side of the mirror it is the literal autobiography of David Copperfield, successful novelist.

On the other hand, the source of the coherence of David's life may be a providential power which has been secretly working behind the scenes to give an objective design to his life. This is suggested by the way the sea, especially in the descriptions of little Em'ly walking on the causeway by the shore and of the storm in which Steerforth and Ham are drowned, becomes a mysterious supernatural reservoir, an external memory and prevision gathering the past and the future together in a time out of time sustained by God. "Is it possible," asks David as he remembers little Em'ly walking so dangerously close to the sea, "among the possibilities of hidden things, that in the sudden rashness of the child and her wild look so far off, there was any merciful attraction of her into danger, any tempting her towards him permitted on the part of her dead father, that her life might have a chance of ending that day?" (35) Later Ham says "the end of it like" seems to him to be coming from the sea (352). In Steerforth's drowning "the inexorable end [comes] at its appointed time" (352). During the storm which is to wash the body of Steerforth up at his feet, David feels that "something within [him], faintly answering to the storm without, tosse[s] up the depths of [his] memory and [makes] a tumult in them" (603). The personal memory within is matched by a cosmic memory without.

The conflict between these two organizing powers is reconciled when David discovers that Agnes has been all along the secret center of his life, the pivot around which everything else will turn out to have been patterning itself as the circle of his life pervaded by her presence. Agnes is the rock on which he can base himself, the person who will fill the void of his old un-

happy loss or want of something. "Clasped in my embrace," says
David after his marriage to Agnes, "I held the source of every
worthy aspiration I had ever had; the centre of myself, the circle
of my life, my own, my wife; my love of whom was founded
on a rock!" (659)

In the last chapter of *David Copperfield* the narrator returns, like the narrator of *Huckleberry Finn,* to the present. The
young David and the grown-up David coincide, and the narrator speaks for his situation in the present. But far from choos-
ing, like Huck, a solitude which is the only guarantee of an
honest life, David has escaped from his solitude into society. He
is surrounded by his family and his friends. Far from speaking,
like Huck, in the voice of solitude on behalf of the values of solitude, he is now and has been throughout the novel as much the
spokesman in the language of the middle-class community for
the values of that community [14] as any of the omniscient narrators of Victorian novels told in the third person—the narrators, for example, of *Vanity Fair, Middlemarch,* or *The Last
Chronicle of Barset* (1866–67). Though the first-person novel
and the third-person novel seem so different, both can become
instruments by which Victorian novelists express their sense that
authentic life lies in assimilation of the individual mind into the
collective mind of society. In marriage to one member of good
middle-class society and in a successful career as a writer of novels, like Dickens himself, David has found a way into that society.

Agnes is also for him the mediator of a heavenly light and a

[14] As opposed to the false upper-class society he describes as "the Desert of
Sahara" (667).

promise of heaven. As such, she is the means by which he sees other things and people, judging them according to universal standards. She is the way in which he will rise through society beyond society, not into the solitude of Huck's "Territory," that lonesomeness lacking any vestige of a divine presence, but into the celestial society of Heaven where he can enjoy Agnes's companionship forever.

Huckleberry Finn is an open-ended fiction. Huck's life is not over on the last page of the novel, and his ability to free himself from Aunt Sally and other agents of "civilization" remains in doubt. Dickens, on the other hand, tries to give *David Copperfield* a closed form. He presents the final sentences of David's narrative as a rehearsal of the final moments of his life. The latter will repeat in structure and content the former, realities fading them as memories fade now. The end of the book is an anticipation of the end of David's life, when there will be no more earthly future left. Like Henry Esmond retelling his life as an old man in Virginia, David speaks as if he were writing from beyond time, as if he were writing from the perspective of death:

> And now, as I close my task, subduing my desire to linger yet, these faces fade away. But one face, shining on me like a Heavenly light by which I see all other objects, is above them and beyond them all. And that remains.
>
> I turn my head, and see it, in its beautiful serenity, beside me. My lamps burns low, and I have written far into the night; but the dear presence, without which I were nothing, bears me company.

Oh Agnes, Oh my soul, so may thy face be by me when I
close my life indeed; so may I, when realities are melting
from me like the shadows which I now dismiss, still find
thee near me, pointing upward! (668, 669)

A modern reader may find it difficult to take seriously the
image of Agnes "pointing upward," and Dickens himself was in
later novels, most subtly in *Our Mutual Friend* (1864–65), to
put in question the strategy by which the conflict between two
sources of order is resolved in *David Copperfield*. The contrast
between Dickens's novel and *Huckleberry Finn,* however, is a
striking example of the different cultural and personal meanings
which may be expressed within the form of the first-person
novel. In Twain's hands the form is used in a masterpiece in the
American tradition of ambiguous personal experience which
goes from Hawthorne and Melville through Twain to Faulkner, Hemingway, and Bellow.

As many critics have seen, Huck speaks not the language of
the community but a pungent vernacular which can thrive only
outside society and is the instrument of a devastating criticism
of it. *Huckleberry Finn,* however, does more than juxtapose two
ways of speaking, one good and one bad. There are three kinds
of language in the novel. Each speaks for a different condition
of life. Existence within society is again and again dramatized as
speaking a false language, playing a role, wearing a disguise,
either wittingly or unwittingly perpetrating a fraud. Honest di-
rectness of speech, on the other hand, is possible only between
Huck and Jim in their ideal society of two on the raft. This
openness and lack of guile is the basis of poignancy in the scene

in which Huck feels guilty for having fooled Jim into believing he has dreamed events which have really happened during a foggy night on the river. "It was fifteen minutes," says Huck, "before I could work myself up to go and humble myself to a nigger—but I done it, and I warn't ever sorry for it afterwards, neither. I didn't do him no more mean tricks, and I wouldn't done that one if I'd knowed it would make him feel that way" (71, 72). Huck's sin is to have imported into the Eden-like honesty of social relations on the raft the propensity for lies which is characteristic of life on the shore and which is, moreover, Huck's only self-defense when he is there. The colloquial rhythm and idiom of his narrative of his life is speech of the raft society. He does his readers the great honor of speaking to them as if they were in collusion with him against the society of the shore and could share with him his true speech.

There is, however, a third language in the novel, a language belonging neither to good society nor to bad society, but to solitude. This language, and the condition belonging to it, are described in two crucial passages in the novel, one near the beginning, when Huck is still living with Miss Watson, and one just before Huck reaches the Phelps Farm and just after he has made his resolution to steal Jim out of slavery again. The same elements occur in both of these passages: an association of isolation with a state of such desolate "lonesomeness" that Huck wishes for death; so complete an openness to inhuman nature and to the presences of the dead within nature that it is as if Huck were already dead; a transformation of language from a means of communication into silence or into an inarticulate murmur, like the speech of elemental nature. The companionship of the dead is a companionship of mute and incommunicable secrets. These texts are of fundamental importance as clues to the quality of Huck's authenticity. They seem clearly related to Twain's deepest sense of his own existence: [15]

> I felt so lonesome [says Huck in the first such passage] I most wished I was dead. . . . [T]he wind was trying to whisper something to me and I couldn't make out what it was, and so it made the cold shivers run over me. Then away out in the woods I heard that kind of a sound that a ghost makes when it wants to tell about something that's on its mind and can't make itself understood, and so can't rest easy in its grave and has to go about that way every night grieving. I got so down-hearted and scared, I did wish I had some company. (8, 9) [16]

Richard Poirier, in *A World Elsewhere,* has noted how often Huck remains speechless when he is with other people on the shore. He is often a silent watcher and listener who effaces himself as much as possible.[17] This silence is an expression of the onlooking detachment from society which is his natural condition and which is affirmed in his resolution at the end to free

[15] These passages were singled out for citation in the earliest recorded review of *Huckleberry Finn,* that by Brander Matthews in the *Saturday Review* [London], January 31, 1885, p. 153.

[16] The second such passage reiterates the motifs of the first and expresses them with equal eloquence: "[T]here was them kind of faint dronings of bugs and flies in the air that makes it seem so lonesome and like everybody's dead and gone; and if a breeze fans along and quivers the leaves, it makes you feel mournful, because you feel like it's spirits whispering—spirits that's been dead ever so many years—and you always think they're talking about *you*. As a general thing it makes a body wish *he* was dead, too, and done with it all" (171).

[17] (New York, 1966), pp. 183–84.

himself from civilization. If Huck chooses for silence and solitude, the book allows the reader no illusion about what these
mean. They mean loss of language and a kinship with the dead.
In solitude one becomes a kind of walking dead man, mute
spectator of life. This, however, is preferable to the intolerable
falsehood of existence within society.

This stark either/or replaces finally the choice between good
society on the raft and bad society on the shore which has apparently structured Huck's narrative. Twain's hesitation before
the darker implications of his story may explain that descent to
the style of *The Adventures of Tom Sawyer* (1876) in the last
episode, so troubling to critics. The Phelps Farm episode, however, plays a strategic role in the progress of the novel. It is the
final stage in a gradual contamination of the honest language of
the raft by the fraudulent language of the shore. In the end,
Huck must choose not between true speech and false speech, but
between speech and silence.

If the temporal structure of the novel brings Huck back to
himself in the present and to the need for a decision there, the
terms of this decision may be identified in its intersubjective
structures. In *Huckleberry Finn* Twain plays the role of Huck
in order to speak indirectly to the real society of his day, just as
he took a pseudonym for his writing, so confronting his readers
in disguise. In this novel he is Samuel Clemens pretending to be
Mark Twain pretending to be Huckleberry Finn. This playing
of roles is also fundamental to the inner structure of the novel,
within the mirror-world its words create. Nothing is more natural to Huck, or more necessary, than lying. Repeatedly he leaves
the "free and easy and comfortable" (95) life on the raft to in-

volve himself in life on the shore. As soon as he meets someone there he spontaneously makes up a whole history for himself, a name, past life, present situation and intention. Only in this way can he protect Jim and that separate part of himself which can hear ghosts and understands what it would be like to be dead. When he enters society he must enter it in disguise, reborn as someone else. To be within the community is to be a fraud, to pretend to be another person, just as in writing the novel Clemens plays the role of Huck. Even the truth must be spoken by way of fiction. Significantly, Huck's final incarnation is as Tom Sawyer, for his greatest danger is that he will become, like Tom, someone who lives his life as a play and is entirely subjected to one form of fiction: the false idols of society and its romantic traditions.

This pattern of person within person, or of person confronting person by way of a disguise, is also a pattern of imaginary and real. If the novel is a fiction by which Twain attempted to approach his childhood and therefore to reach his own inmost reality, the story itself is constructed as a design of fictions within fictions—the fictions of Huck's lies and disguises, the fictional world taken from novels and historical romances within which Tom Sawyer lives, the no less fictional structures of religious and social beliefs which entrance the Mississippi communities, the frauds perpetrated by the duke and the king. In the travesties of *Hamlet* and *Romeo and Juliet* by the latter, they pretend to be a king and a duke pretending to be the famous actors Garrick and Kean pretending to be Shakespearean characters. These fictions within fictions keep before the reader a picture of interpersonal relations as a complex system of deceit within deceit in which every man lies to his neighbor.

The theme of lies leads back to the paradox of Huck's own language. As Ernest Hemingway, T. S. Eliot, and others have said, Huck's speech is the basis of the book's authenticity. He uses a rich vernacular idiom, couched in indigenous American rhythms, vocabulary, and syntax. His speech grows out of the way of life of a people in a place, and therefore is rooted in reality in a way no abstract language can be. At the same time the novel is full of demonstrations of the hollowness of the language spoken by people around Huck. This is most apparent in the vigorous satires of religious language, but it is also present in the satire of Southern romanticism in the references to Sir Walter Scott and *Lalla Rookh* (both names of steamboats in the novel). A similar theme is expressed in the imprisonment of the Grangerfords and Shepherdsons in linguistic molds which keep their absurd feud going from generation to generation. To belong to Mississippi Valley society is to be unable to speak the truth, to use one form or another of a fantasy language which justifies the greatest cruelties and injustices—slavery, economic exploitation, and the arrogant self-righteousness and psychological cruelties practiced, in Twain's view, in the name of Protestant Christianity.

Though Huck's language is a speech within the community speech, one based partly on the folklore and linguistic vigor of children and Negroes, nevertheless it has grown out of the community language and remains part of it. If it has drawn its strength from its source, it must share also the weaknesses of its origin. Huck's style comes from the popular culture of the Mississippi, but the novel is the exposure of that culture by way of its imitation in its own words. This use of the destructive power of imitative language reveals the silent presence of Twain be-

hind Huck, of the lonesome and silent Huck behind his participation in his culture.

When Huck speaks he too gets caught in the speech patterns of his society. This is apparent in the irony of those many
places where the reader can glimpse Twain judging Huck, de-
ploring his enslavement to a false rhetoric. An example is the
famous passage in which Huck, in response to a question about
whether anyone was killed in a steamboat explosion, says,
"No'm. Killed a nigger" (173). The poignant ambiguity of the
crucial text in which Huck decides to rescue Jim from slavery
lies in the fact that he is forced to express his decision in the
language of the culture surrounding him. He must use religious
and social terms which reverse Twain's judgment of good and
bad in the situation. Worse yet, he is forced to experience the
feelings appropriate to the rhetoric of the language he must use
because he has no other. As long as he is within society he remains trapped in its language. However he acts, his actions are
defined in the community's terms.

Twain and his readers may see in Huck's resolve a heroic
act of moral improvisation, an intuition of the truth like that
described in W. E. H. Lecky's *History of European Morals from
Augustus to Charlemagne* (1869), a book Twain admired.
Such a reading sees in Huck the courage to act in accordance
with an intuititively perceived moral truth even though it goes
counter to the rules of a bad society. Huck, however, does not
see it that way at all. He sees his decision to free Jim as the victory of his innate evil over the good teaching of society. It is a
conscious choice of damnation. To him it is not the creation of a
just moral order in place of the evil one supported by society.

His decision to "take up wickedness again" is reprehensible defiance of community laws defending religious right and the sanctity of private property. His act is not a "yes" in obedience to a higher ethical law but a "no" to the yes of a community which he continues to accept. "I was a trembling," says Huck, "because I'd got to decide, forever, betwixt two things, and I knowed it. I studied a minute, sort of holding my breath, and then says to myself: 'All right, then, I'll *go* to hell'" (168).

Even if Huck succeeds in freeing Jim, this freedom is still a social condition. As the concluding episode of Tom's "evasion" of Jim shows, Jim is as much subject to the sham of his society when he is free as when he is a slave. Only complete isolation is freedom. This is the meaning of the absurdity of Tom's freeing Jim when he is already legally free. Free man or slave, he is still enslaved, like Tom, Aunt Sally, and the rest, by the linguistic and cultural patterns of his society. To negate these is still to remain within them, and so to affirm them indirectly. Whenever Huck speaks he is necessarily subject to this inexorable law. To speak at all he must speak lies, not only because his situation forces him to deception, disguise, play-acting, but because the language of his community is inevitably the instrument of lies. The truth cannot be spoken directly in it, as Huck proves in the soliloquy of his decision to rescue Jim. The choice Huck faces is therefore between false language and no language at all. And this corresponds to the choice between participation in a false society and an isolation from other people which is like death.[18] Society is always imaginary. Solitude is the way to the real.

[18] Kenneth S. Lynn, in *Mark Twain and Southwestern Humor* (Boston, 1959), p. 245, notes the relevance to this theme of the fact that one of the many sequels

Huck's final resolution, his final integrity, is a choice of lonesomeness and the silence which goes with it: "[S]o there ain't nothing more to write about, and I am rotten glad of it, because if I'd a knowed what a trouble it was to make a book I wouldn't a tackled it and ain't agoing to no more" (226). Then follows his decision to "light out for the Territory ahead of the rest."

To explore in a given novel temporal, interpersonal, and representational structures will lead to an identification of the specific shaping energy which generates form and meaning in the novel in question: the reaffirmation in *David Copperfield,* against alternative possibilities, of a traditional transcendentalism, or the rejection of society and its languages which in *Huckleberry Finn* prepares for the more overt nihilism of Satan's scorn for the "moral sense" in *The Mysterious Stranger* (1916).

Twain contemplated for *Huckleberry Finn* "envisioned Huck as a broken, helplessly insane old man."

DICKENS AND THE COMEDY OF HUMORS

~~~ DICKENS PRESENTS SPECIAL PROBLEMS to any critic
who approaches him in the context of a "Victorian
novelist." In general, the serious Victorian fiction writers are
realistic and the less serious ones are romancers. We expect
George Eliot or Trollope to give us a solid and well-rounded
realization of the social life, attitudes, and intellectual issues of
their time: we expect Disraeli and Bulwer-Lytton, because they
are more "romantic," to give us the same kind of thing in a
more flighty and dilettantish way; from the cheaper brands,
Marie Corelli or Ouida, we expect nothing but the standard romance formulas. This alignment of the serious and the realistic,
the commercial and the romantic, where realism has a moral
dignity that romance lacks, intensified after Dickens's death,
survived through the first half of the twentieth century, and still
lingers vestigially. But in such an alignment Dickens is hard to
place. What he writes, if I may use my own terminology for
once, are not realistic novels but fairy tales in the low mimetic
displacement. Hence there has grown up an assumption that, if
we are to take Dickens seriously, we must emphasize the lifelikeness of his characters or the shrewdness of his social observation; if we emphasize his violently unplausible plots and his

playing up of popular sentiment, we are emphasizing only his
concessions to an undeveloped public taste. This was a contemporary view of him, expressed very lucidly by Trollope in *The
Warden,* and it is still a natural one to take.

A refinement of the same view sees the real story in Dickens's novels as a rather simple set of movements within a large
group of characters. To this a mechanical plot seems to have
been attached like an outboard motor to a rowboat, just to get
things moving faster and more noisily. Thus our main interest,
in reading *Little Dorrit,* is in the straightforward and quite
touching story of Clennam's love for the heroine, of their sep-
aration through her suddenly acquired wealth, and of their
eventual reunion through her loss of it. Along with this goes a
preposterous melodrama about forged wills, identical twins, a
mother who is not a mother, skulking foreigners, and dark mysteries of death and birth which seems almost detachable from
the central story. Similarly, we finish *Our Mutual Friend* with a
clear memory of a vast panoramic pageant of Victorian society,
from the nouveau-riche Veneerings to Hexham living on the refuse of the Thames. But the creaky Griselda plot, in which John
Harmon pretends to be dead in order to test the stability of his
future wife, is something that we can hardly take in even when
reading the book, much less remember afterwards.

Some works of fiction present a clearly designed or projected plot, where each episode seems to us to be logically the se-
quel to the previous episode. In others we feel that the episode
that comes next does so only because the author has decided that
it will come next. In stories with a projected plot we explain
the episode from its context in the plot; in stories lacking such a

plot, we are often thrown back on some other explanation, often one that originates in the author's wish to tell us something besides the story. This last is particularly true of thematic sequences like the "Dream Play" of Strindberg, where the succession of episodes is not like that of a projected plot, nor particularly like a dream either, but has to be accounted for in different terms. In Dickens we often notice that when he is most actively pursuing his plot he is careless, to the verge of being contemptuous, of the inner logic of the story. In *Little Dorrit,* the mysterious rumblings and creakings in the Clennam house, referred to at intervals throughout, mean that it is about to fall down. What this in turn means is that Dickens is going to push it over at a moment when the villain is inside and the hero outside. Similarly, Clennam, after a good deal of detective work, manages to discover where Miss Wade is living on the Continent. She did not expect him to ferret out her address, nor had she anything to say to him when he arrived; but, just in case he did come, she had written out the story of her life and had kept it in a drawer ready to hand to him. The outrage on probability seems almost deliberate, as does the burning up of Krook in *Bleak House* by spontaneous combustion as soon as the author is through with him, despite Dickens's protests about the authenticity of his device. Dickens's daughter, Mrs. Pellegrini, remarked shrewdly that there was no reason to suppose that *The Mystery of Edwin Drood* would have been any more of an impeccable plot-structure than the novels that Dickens had already completed. But, because it is unfinished, the plot has been the main focus of critical attention in that story, usually on the assumption that this once Dickens was working with a plot which was not, like a fictional Briareus, equipped with a hundred arms of coincidence.

T. S. Eliot, in his essay on Dickens and Wilkie Collins, remarks on the "spurious fatality" of Collins's detective-story plots. This is no place to raise the question of why the sense of fatality in *The Moonstone* should be more spurious than in *The Family Reunion,* but we notice in Dickens how strong the impulse is to reject a logicality inherent in the story in favor of impressing on the reader an impatient sense of absolutism: of saying, in short, *la fatalité, c'est moi.* This disregard of plausibility is worth noticing, because everyone realizes that Dickens is a great genius of the absurd in his characterization, and it is possible that his plots are also absurd in the same sense, not from incompetence or bad taste, but from a genuinely creative instinct. If so, they are likely to be more relevant to the entire conception of the novel than is generally thought. I proceed to explore a little the sources of absurdity in Dickens, to see if that will lead us to a clearer idea of his total structure.

The structure that Dickens uses for his novels is the New Comedy structure, which has come down to us from Plautus and Terence through Ben Jonson, an author we know Dickens admired, and Molière. The main action is a collision of two societies which we may call for convenience the obstructing and the congenial society. The congenial society is usually centered on the love of hero and heroine, the obstructing society on the characters, often parental, who try to thwart this love. For most of the action the thwarting characters are in the ascendant, but toward the end a twist in the plot reverses the situation and the congenial society dominates the happy ending. A frequent form

of plot-reversal was the discovery that one of the central characters, usually the heroine, was of better social origin than pre-
viously thought. This theme of mysterious parentage is greatly
expanded in the late Greek romances, which closely resemble
some of the plots of Menander. Here an infant of noble birth
may be stolen or exposed and brought up by humble foster-
parents, being restored to his original status at the end. In
drama such a theme involves expounding a complicated ante-
cedent action, and however skillfully done not all audiences
have the patience to follow the unraveling, as Ben Jonson dis-
covered to his cost at the opening of his *New Inn*. But in narrative forms, of course, it can have room to expand. Shakespeare
gets away with it in *The Winter's Tale* by adopting a narrative-
paced form of drama, where sixteen years are encompassed by
the action.

Dickens is, throughout his career, very conventional in his
handling of the New Comedy plot structure. All the stock devices, listed in Greek times as laws, oaths, compacts, witnesses,
and ordeals, can be found in him. *Oliver Twist* and *Edwin
Drood* are full of oaths, vows, councils of war, and conspiracies,
on both benevolent and sinister sides. Witnesses include eaves-
droppers like the Newman Noggs of *Nicholas Nickleby* or
Morfin the cello-player in *Dombey and Son*. Ordeals are of various kinds: near-fatal illnesses are common, and we may compare
the way that information is extracted from Rob the Grinder by
Mrs. Brown in *Dombey and Son* with the maltreating of the
tricky slave in Menander and Plautus. Many thrillers (perhaps
a majority) use a stock episode of having the hero entrapped by
the villain, who instead of killing him at once imparts an essen-

tial piece of information about the plot to him, after which the hero escapes, gaining his wisdom at the price of an ordeal of facing death. This type of episode occurs in *Great Expectations* in the encounter with Orlick.

Every novel of Dickens is a comedy (N.B.: such words as "comedy" are not essence words but context words, hence this means: "for every novel of Dickens the obvious context is comedy"). The death of a central character does not make a story tragic, any more than a similar device does in *The King and I* or *The Yeomen of the Guard*. Sydney Carton is a man without a social function who achieves that function by sacrificing himself for the congenial society; Little Nell's death is so emotionally luxurious that it provides a kind of muted festivity for the conclusion, or what *Finnegans Wake* calls a "funferall." The emphasis at the end of a comedy is sometimes thrown, not on the forming of a new society around the marriage of hero and heroine, but on the maturing or enlightening of the hero, a process which may detach him from marriage or full participation in the congenial group. We find this type of conclusion in Shaw's *Candida*: Dickens's contribution to it is *Great Expectations*. Again, there is usually a mystery in Dickens's stories, and this mystery is nearly always the traditional mystery of birth, in sharp contrast to the mystery of death on which the modern whodunit is based. In Dickens, when a character is murdered, we usually see it done, and if not the suspense is still perfunctory. A detective appears in *Bleak House* to investigate the murder of Tulkinghorn, but his task is easy: Lady Dedlock keeps a French maid, and French maids, being foreign, are emotionally unpredictable and morally insensitive. The problem is much less interesting than the problem of Lady Dedlock's guilty secret, which involves a birth. Unless Edwin Drood was very unlike Dickens's other heroes, the mystery about him is much more likely to have been a mystery of how he got into the world than of how he disappeared from it.

The emergence of the congenial society at the conclusion of the story is presented in the traditional New Comedy terms of festivity. It usually holds several marriages; it dispenses money if it has money, and it dispenses a good deal of food. Such features have remained unchanged in the New Comedy tradition since Greek times. Dickens's predilection for feasting scenes needs no laboring: it may be significant that his last written words are "falls to with an appetite." This feature accounts for his relentless plugging of Christmas, always for him the central symbol of the congenial family feast. The famous sentimentality of Dickens is largely confined to demonstrations of family affection, and is particularly evident in certain set scenes that immediately precede the dénouement, where the affection of brother and sister, of father and daughter, or more rarely of mother and son, is the main theme. Examples are the housekeeping of Tom and Ruth Pinch in *Martin Chuzzlewit,* the dinner of Kit and his mother in *The Old Curiosity Shop,* the meetings of Bella Wilfer with her father in *Our Mutual Friend*. Such relationships, though occasionally described as marriages, are "innocent" in the technical Victorian sense of not involving sexual intercourse, and if they seem to post-Freudian readers to be emotionally somewhat overcharged, it is because they contribute to, and anticipate, the final triumph of Eros at the end of the story. The disregard of plausibility, already mentioned, is another traditional feature, being part of the violent manipulation of the story in the direction of a happy ending. Those who object to such endings on the grounds of probability are often put in the position of questioning the ways of divine providence, which uses the author as its agent for vindicating virtue and baffling vice.

Most of the people who move across the pages of Dickens are neither realistic portraits, like the characters of Trollope, nor "caricatures," so far as that term implies only a slightly different approach to realistic portraiture. They are humors, like the characters in Ben Jonson, who formulated the principle that humors were the appropriate characters for a New Comedy plot. The humor is a character identified with a characteristic, like the miser, the hypochondriac, the braggart, the parasite, or the pedant. He is obsessed by whatever it is that makes him a humor, and the sense of our superiority to an obsessed person, someone bound to an invariable ritual habit, is, according to Bergson, one of the chief sources of laughter. But it is not because he is incidentally funny that the humor is important in New Comedy: he is important because his obsession is the feature that creates the conditions of the action, and the opposition of the two societies. In *The Silent Woman,* everything depends on Morose's hatred of noise; covetousness and gullibility set everything going in *Volpone* and *The Alchemist* respectively. Thus it is only the obstructing society which is "humorous," in the Jonsonian sense, as a society. In Dickens we find humors on both sides of the social conflict, genial, generous, and lovable humors as well as absurd or sinister ones. But the humors in the congenial society merely diversify it with amiable and harmless eccentricities; the humors of the obstructing society help to build up that society, with all its false standards and values.

Most of the standard types of humor are conspicuous in Dickens, and could be illustrated from *Bleak House* alone: the miser in Smallweed; the hypocrite in Chadband; the parasite in Skimpole and Turveydrop; the pedant in Mrs. Jellyby. The braggart soldier is not much favored: Major Bagstock in *Dombey and Son* is more of a parasite. Agreeably to the conditions of Victorian life, the braggart soldier is replaced by a braggart merchant or politician. An example, treated in a thoroughly traditional manner, is Bounderby in *Hard Times.* Another Victorian commonplace of the braggart-soldier family, the duffer sportsman, whose pretensions are far beyond his performance, is represented by Winkle in *The Pickwick Papers.* There are, however, two Winkles in *The Pickwick Papers,* the duffer sportsman and the pleasant young man who breaks down family opposition on both sides to acquire a pleasant young woman. The duality reflects the curious and instructive way that *The Pickwick Papers* came into being. The original scheme proposed to Dickens was a comedy of humors in its most primitive and superficial form: a situation comedy in which various stock types, including an incautious amorist (Tupman), a melancholy poet (Snodgrass), and a pedant (Pickwick), as well as Winkle, get into one farcical predicament after another. This form is frequent in stories for children, and was represented in my childhood by now obsolete types of comic strip and silent movie comedies. It must have left some descendants in television, but my impression is that contemporary children are deficient in this vitamin. But although traces of the original

scheme persist throughout *The Pickwick Papers,* it quickly
turns inside out into a regular New Comedy story, which leads
up in the regular way to a recognition scene and a reversal of
direction in the plot at its most serious point, in the debtors'
prison. The pedant becomes a man of principle, and the humor
of pedantry is transferred to the law which entraps him. Thus
the comedy of humors takes root in society, as Dickens sees society, instead of merely extending from one incident to another.

The simplest form of humor is the tagged humor, who is
associated with the repetition of a set phrase. Thus we have Mrs.
Micawber, whose tag is that she will never desert Mr. Micawber,
and Major Bagnet in *Bleak House,* who admires his wife but
asserts that he never tells her so because "discipline must be
maintained." We notice that our sense of superiority to such
characters is edged with antagonism: when the repeated trait is
intended to be endearing we are more likely to find it irritating,
as E. M. Forster does Mrs. Micawber's. Jarndyce with his "east
wind" tag and Esther Summerson's constant bewilderment that
other people should find her charming do not stick in our
minds in the way that Chadband and Mrs. Jellyby do. The
humor is, almost by definition, a bore, and the technical skill in
handling him consists in seeing that we get just enough but not
too much of him. The more unpleasant he is, the easier this
problem is to solve. Repetition which is excessive even by
Dickensian standards, like the emphasis on Carker's teeth in
Dombey and Son, is appropriate for a villain, as its effect is to
dehumanize and cut off sympathy. We cannot feel much concern over the fate of a character who is presented to us mainly
as a set of teeth, like Berenice in Poe. The "lifelikeness" of a

humor depends on two things: on the fact that we are all very largely creatures of ritual habit, and on the strength of a perverse tendency in most of us to live up to our own caricatures. Pecksniff may be a humbug, but that can hardly be the whole of our feeling about him when he begins to sound like a member of my own profession attempting to extract a discussion from a group of clammed-up freshmen:

> "The name of those fabulous animals (pagan, I regret to say) who used to sing in the water, has quite escaped me."
>
> Mr. George Chuzzlewit suggested "Swans."
>
> "No," said Mr. Pecksniff. "Not swans. Very like swans, too. Thank you."
>
> The nephew with the outline of a countenance, speaking for the first and last time on that occasion, propounded "Oysters."
>
> "No," said Mr. Pecksniff, with his own peculiar urbanity, "nor oysters. But by no means unlike oysters: a very excellent idea; thank you, my dear sir, very much. Wait! Sirens. Dear me! sirens, of course."

Humors are, at least dramatically, "good" if they are on the side of the congenial society, "bad" or ridiculous if on the side of the obstructing one. Thus the humor comedy has an easy and natural connection with the morality play. We notice this in the allegorical names that Dickens often gives some of his minor characters, like the "Pyke" and "Pluck" who are the satellites of Sir Mulberry Hawk in *Nicholas Nickleby,* or the "Bar," "Bishop," and "Physician" who turn up at Merdle's dinners in *Little Dorrit*. We notice it also in Dickens's tendency to arrange his humors in moral pairs, whether both are in the same novel or not. As just indicated, we have a "good" major in *Bleak House* and a "bad" one with a very similar name in *Dombey and Son;* we have a villainous Jew in *Oliver Twist* and a saintly Jew in *Our Mutual Friend,* and so on. Within *Dombey and Son* itself the "bad" major is paired against a "good" navy man, Captain Cuttle. If characters change sides, there may be a metamorphosis of character, which is not difficult in the humor technique, because it simply means putting on a different mask. Thus the generous Boffin pretends to be a miser for a while; Scrooge goes through the reverse process; Mercy Pecksniff changes roles from the feather-head to the faithful ill-used wife, and so on. Many humors are really chorus characters, who cannot do anything in the plot unless they step out of their roles: an example is Lord Frederick Verisopht in *Nicholas Nickleby,* who has to harden up a good deal to make his tragic end appropriate. The commonest form of this metamorphosis, and the most traditional one, is the release of the humor from his obsession at the end of the story: through the experience gained in the story, he is able to break through his besetting fault. At the end of *Martin Chuzzlewit* there is a whole series of these changes: the hero escapes from his selfishness, Mark Tapley from his compulsion to search for difficult situations in order to "come out strong," and Tom Pinch from an innocence that Dickens recognizes to be more obsessive than genuine innocence, and which we should now think of as a streak of masochism.

The rhetoric of the tagged humor consists mainly of variations of the stock identifying phrase or phrases. Some humors acquire a personal rhetorical rhythm of a strongly associative kind, which because it is associative gives the effect of being obsessive. The disjointed phrases of Jingle and the asyntactic babble of Mrs. Nickleby and Flora Finching are perhaps the most consistently successful examples. Closer to the single identifying phrase are Uriah Heep's insistence on his "'umble" qualities, which reminds us a little of Iago's "honest" tag, and the repetitions that betray the hypocrisy of Casby, the squeezing landlord in *Little Dorrit*. Others develop parodies of standard types of oratory, like Chadband with his parsonical beggar's whine or Micawber with his Parliamentary flourishes.

More significant, for a reason that will meet us in a moment, is the humor of stock response, that is, the humor whose obsession it is to insist that what he or she has been conditioned to think proper and acceptable is in fact reality. This attitude gives us the Bouvard-et-Pécuchet type of humor, whose mind is confined within a dictionary of accepted ideas. Such humors, it is obvious, readily expand into cultural allegories, representatives of the kind of anxiety that caricatures an age. Thus our stereotypes about "Victorian prudery" are represented by Podsnap in *Our Mutual Friend* and Mrs. General (the prunes-and-prisms woman) in *Little Dorrit*. Martin Chuzzlewit finds that America is full of such humors: American shysters are no better and no worse than their British counterparts, but there is a more theoretical element in their lying, and bluster about their enlightened political institutions is much more used as a cover for swindling. In America, in other words, the complacent Podsnap and the rascally Lammle are more likely to be associated in the same person. The implication, which Dickens is not slow to press, is that American life is more vulnerable than British life to character assassination, personal attacks, charges of being un-American, and mob violence. A humor of this stock-response type is comic on Freudian principles: he often says what more cautious people would not say, but show by their actions that they believe. Thus Bumble's remarks about "them wicious paupers" are funny, not as typical of a Victorian beadle, but as revealing the hatred and contempt for the poor that official charity attempts to disguise.

Sometimes a humor's obsessed behavior and repetitive speech suggest a puppet or mechanical doll, whose response is invariable whatever the stimulus. We may feel with some of these characters that the mechanical quality is simply the result of Dickens's not having worked hard enough on them, but occasionally we realize that Dickens himself is encouraging us to see them as inanimate objects. Wemmick the postbox in *Great Expectations,* Pancks the "tug" in *Little Dorrit,* and several characters who are figuratively and to some extent literally wooden, like Silas Wegg, are examples. The Captain Cuttle of *Dombey and Son,* in particular, impresses us as an animated version of the Wooden Midshipman over the shop he so often inhabits. In *The Old Curiosity Shop,* after we have been introduced to Quilp, Little Nell and her grandfather set out on their travels and see a Punch and Judy show. It occurs to us that Quilp, who is described as a "grotesque puppet," who lies, cheats, beats his wife, gets into fistfights, drinks like a salamander, and comes to a sticky end in a bog, *is* Punch, brought to life as a character. Wyndham Lewis, in an essay on Joyce (another admirer of Ben Jonson), notes the Dickensian ancestry of Bloom's interior monologue in the speech of Jingle. He might have noted a similar connection between Flora Finching's unpunctuated harangues in *Little Dorrit* and the reverie of Molly Bloom. Lewis in his turn developed, mainly out of Bergson, a theory of satire as a vision of human behavior in mechanical terms, where his main predecessor, if not one he recognized, was Dickens. We notice also the reappearance of the Punch figure in the center of *The Human Age.*

We noted that, while there are humors on both sides of the social conflict in Dickens, it is only the obstructing society which is humorous as a society. This takes us back to the feature I mentioned at the beginning which distinguishes Dickens from his major contemporaries in fiction. In most of the best Victorian novels, apart from Dickens, the society described is organized by its institutions: the church, the government, the professions, the rural squirearchy, business, and the trade unions. It is a highly structured society, and the characters function from within those structures. But in Dickens we get a much more freewheeling and anarchistic social outlook. For him the structures of society, as structures, belong almost entirely to the absurd, obsessed, sinister aspect of it, the aspect that is overcome or evaded by the comic action. The comic action itself moves toward the regrouping of society around the only social unit that Dickens really regards as genuine, the family. In other Victorian novelists characters are regrouped within their social structures; in Dickens the comic action leads to a sense of having broken down or through those structures. Naturally there are limits to this: the same social functions have to continue; but the sense that social institutions have to reverse their relationship to human beings before society really becomes congenial is very strong.

The law, for instance, as represented by the Chancery suit in

Bleak House and the Circumlocution Office in *Little Dorrit,* is a kind of social vampire, sucking out family secrets or draining off money through endless shifts and evasions. It is explicitly said in both novels that the legal establishment is not designed to be an instrument of society, but to be a self-perpetuating social parasite. Education, again, is usually presented in Dickens as a racket, a brutal and malignant racket with Squeers and Creakle, a force-feeding racket in the "fact" school of *Hard Times* and the Classical cram school of Dr. Blimber in *Dombey and Son.* Dickens's view of the liberalizing quality of the Victorian Classical training is perhaps symbolized in the grotesque scenes of Silas Wegg stumbling through Gibbon's *Decline and Fall* to the admiration of the illiterate Boffins: an unskillful performance which nobody understands. As for religion, even the respectable churches have little to do except marry the hero and heroine, and the spokesmen of the chapel, Chadband and Stiggins, are the same type of greasy lout as their ancestor in Ben Jonson, Zeal-of-the-Land Busy. Politics, from the Eatanswill election in *Pickwick* to the Parliamentary career of Veneering in *Our Mutual Friend,* is a farce, only tolerable when an amusing one. Industry is equally repulsive whether its spokesman is Bounderby or the labor organizer Slackbridge. The amassing of a fortune in the City, by Dombey, Ralph Nickleby, or Merdle in *Little Dorrit,* is an extension of miserliness: it is closely associated with usury; the debtor's prison is clearly the inseparable other side of it, and it usually blows up a bubble of credit speculation with no secured assets, ending in an appalling financial crash and endless misery. *Martin Chuzzlewit* carefully balances the swindling of American real estate speculators with the precisely similar activities of Montague's Anglo-Bengalee Company in London. In several of the novels there are two obstructing societies, one a social establishment and the other a criminal anti-establishment. When this occurs there is little if anything morally to choose between them. We find the Artful Dodger no worse than the respectable Bumble in his beadle's uniform, and Pip discovers a human companionship with the hunted convict on the marshes that the Wopsles and Pumblechooks of his Christmas dinner exclude him from.

It is perhaps in *Little Dorrit* that we get the most complete view of the obstructing society, a society which is shown to be a self-imprisoning society, locking itself in to the invariable responses of its own compulsions. At the beginning we are introduced to various types of prison: the Marseilles prison with Blandois, the quarantine prison with the discontented Tattycoram and her Lesbian familiar Miss Wade, the prison-house of the paralyzed Mrs. Clennam, and finally the Marshalsea. As the story goes on these external prisons give place to internal ones. With the Circumlocution Office the prison image modulates to a maze or labyrinth, a very frequent sinister image in Dickens, and gradually a unified vision of the obstructing society takes shape. This society is symbolized by the Barnacles, who, as their name indicates, represent a social parasitism inherent in the aristocracy, and operating through the political and legal establishment. They are a family, but not a genuine family: their loyalties are class or tribal loyalties cutting across the real structure of society. One of their members, Mrs. Gowan, even goes so far as to speak of marriage as "accidental," and stresses the primary necessity of defending the position of her class, or rather of her private myth about her class. The fact that her son becomes the husband of the only child of the Meagles family gives a most ambiguous twist to the happy ending of the novel. We may compare the disaster wrought by Steerforth in *David Copperfield,* whose mother is similarly obsessed with making her son into a symbol of class arrogance. We begin to understand how consistent the pitiful pretense of aristocracy that old Dorrit tries to maintain, first in the prison, then in prosperity, is with the general scheme of the story. Miss Wade's autobiography, headed "The History of a Self-Tormentor," however arbitrarily introduced into the story, has a genuine symbolic relevance to it, and one of the most sharply observed passages in the novel is the moment of self-awareness when Fanny Dorrit realizes that her own selfishness is implacably driving her into an endless, pointless, pleasureless game of one-upmanship with Mrs. Merdle. Similarly in *Great Expectations* the "gentleman's" world which entraps Pip is symbolized by the decaying prison-house where all the clocks have been stopped at the moment of Miss Havisham's humiliation, the rest of her life consisting only of brooding on that moment.

The obstructing society in Dickens has two main characteristics: it is parasitic and it is pedantic. It is parasitic in the sense of setting up false values and loyalties which destroy the freedom of all those who accept them, as well as tyrannizing over many of those who do not. Dickens's implicit social vision is also radical, to an extent he hardly realized himself, in dividing society between workers and idlers, and in seeing in much of the leisure class a social sanctioning of parasitism. As for its pedantry, it is traditional in New Comedy to set up a pragmatic

standard, based on experience, as a norm, and contrast it with
the theoretical approaches to life typical of humors who cannot
escape from their reflex responses. Like Blake, like every writer
with any genuine radicalism in him, Dickens finds the really
dangerous social evils in those which have achieved some acceptance by being rationalized. Already in *Oliver Twist* the
word "experience" stands as a contrast to the words "experi-
mental" and "philosophical," which are invariably pejorative.
This contrast comes into Bumble's famous "the law is a ass"
speech. In *Hard Times* the pedantry of the obstructing society is
associated with a utilitarian philosophy and an infantile trust in
facts, statistics, and all impersonal and generalized forms of
knowledge. We may wonder why Dickens denounces this philosophy so earnestly and caricatures it so crudely, instead of let-
ting its absurdities speak for themselves. But it is clear that *Hard
Times,* of all Dickens's stories, comes nearest to being what in
our day is sometimes called the dystopia, the book which, like
Brave New World or *1984,* shows us the nightmare world that
results from certain perverse tendencies inherent in society getting free play. The most effective dystopias are likely to be those
in which the author isolates certain features in his society that
most directly threaten his own social function as a writer.
Dickens sees in the cult of facts and statistics a threat, not to the
realistic novelist, and not only to a life based on concrete and
personal relations, but to the unfettered imagination, the mind
that can respond to fairy tales and fantasy and understand their
relevance to reality. The insistence on the importance of fairy
tales, nursery rhymes, and similar genres in education often
meets us in Dickens, and implies that Dickens's fairy-tale plots

are regarded by Dickens himself as an essential part of his novels.

The action of a comedy moves toward an identity which is usually a social identity. In Dickens the family, or a group analogous to a family, is the key to social identity. Hence his recognition scenes are usually genealogical, concerned with discovering unknown fathers and mothers or articulating the correct family relationships. There are often three sets of parental figures attached to a central character, with several doubles of each. First are the actual parents. These are often dead before the story begins, like the fathers of Nicholas Nickleby and David Copperfield, or stagger on weakly for a few pages, like David Copperfield's mother, or are mysterious and emerge at the end, sometimes as bare names unrelated to the story, like Oliver Twist's father or the parents of Little Nell. The father of Sissy Jupe in *Hard Times* deserts her without ever appearing in the novel; the first things we see in *Great Expectations* are the tombstones of Pip's parents. Pip himself is brought up by a sister who is twenty years older and (as we learn on practically the last page of the book) has the same name as his mother. Next come the parental figures of the obstructing society, generally cruel or foolish, and often descended from the harsh stepparents of folktale. Murdstone and his sister, Pip's sister, the pseudo-mothers of Esther Summerson and Clennam, belong to this group. One very frequent device which combines these two types of relationship is that of the preternaturally loving and hard-working daughter who is the sole support of a weak or foolish father. We have, among others, Little Dorrit, Little Nell, whose grandfather is a compulsive gambler, Jenny Wren in *Our*

Mutual Friend with her drunken "child," Madeline Bray in *Nicholas Nickleby,* and, in a different way, Florence Dombey. Naturally the marriage of such a heroine, following on the death of the parent, transfers her to the more congenial society. Finally we have the parental or avuncular figures of the congenial society itself, those who take on a protective relation to the central characters as the story approaches its conclusion. Brownlow in *Oliver Twist,* who adopts the hero, Jarndyce in *Bleak House,* Abel Magwitch in *Great Expectations,* the Cheeryble brothers in *Nicholas Nickleby,* the Boffins in *Our Mutual Friend,* are examples. Abel Magwitch, besides being the ultimate father of Pip, is also the actual father of Estella, which makes Estella in a sense Pip's sister: this was doubtless one reason why Dickens so resisted the conventional ending of marriage for these two. The more realistic developments of New Comedy tend to eliminate this genealogical apparatus. When one of the girls in *Les Précieuses Ridicules* announces that being so interesting a girl she is quite sure that her real parents are much more interesting people than the ones she appears to have, we do not take her very seriously. But Dickens is always ready to co-operate with the lonely child's fantasies about lost congenial parents, and this marks his affinity with the romantic side of the tradition, the side related to Classical romance.

I have used the word "anarchistic" in connection with Dickens's view of society, but it is clear that, so far as his comic structure leads to any sort of vision of a social ideal, that ideal would have to be an intensely paternalistic society, an expanded family. We get a somewhat naïve glimpse of this with the Cheeryble brothers in *Nicholas Nickleby,* giving a party where the faithful servitors are brought in at the end for a drink of champagne, expresssing undying loyalty and enthusiasm for the patronizing social arrangements. The reader gets the uneasy feeling that he is listening to the commercial. When in *Little Dorrit* Tattycoram runs away from the suffocating geniality of the Meagles family she has to be brought back repentant, though she may well have had much more of the reader's sympathy than Dickens intended her to have. Even the Dedlock ménage in *Bleak House,* hopeless social anachronism as Dickens clearly recognizes it to be, is still close enough to a family to gather a fair amount of the society of the novel around it at the end. In contrast, social parasites often assume the role of a false father. Examples include the Marquis in *A Tale of Two Cities* whose assassin is technically guilty of parricide, Sir Joseph Bowley, the Urizenic friend and father of the poor in *The Chimes,* and the elder Chester in *Barnaby Rudge.*

In New Comedy the obstructing humors absorb most of the character interest: the heroes and heroines are seldom individualized. Such characters as Bonario in *Volpone* or Valère in *Tartuffe* are only pleasant young men. In Dickens too the heroes and heroines resemble humors only in the fact that their responses are predictable, but they are predictable in terms of a norm, and they seldom if ever appear in the ridiculous or self-binding role of the humor. Such characters, who encourage the reader to identify with them, and who might be called norm-figures, could not exist in serious twentieth-century fiction, which belongs to the ironic mode, and sees all its characters as affected in some degree by hampering social forces. But they have some validity in nineteenth-century low mimetic conventions, which present only what is conventionally presentable, and whose heroes and heroines may therefore logically be models of presentability.

Comedy usually depicts the triumph of the young over the old, but Dickens is unusual among comic writers in that so many of his heroes and heroines are children, or are described in ways that associate them with childhood. Nobody has described more vividly than Dickens the reactions of a sensitive child in a Brobdingnagian world dominated by noisome and blundering adults. And because nearly all these children are predestined to belong to the congenial society, they can only be hurt, not corrupted, by the obstructing society. The one striking exception is Pip, whose detachment from the false standards of the obstructing group forms the main theme of *Great Expectations.* But David Copperfield is only superficially affected by his environment, and Oliver Twist escapes from the activities of the Fagin gang as miraculously as Marina does from the brothel in Shakespeare's *Pericles.* Usually this predestined child-figure is a girl. Many of the heroines, even when grown women, are described as "little" or are compared to fairies. A frequent central theme in Dickens is the theme of *Alice in Wonderland:* the descent of the invulnerable girl-child into a grotesque world. In the preface to *The Old Curiosity Shop* Dickens speaks of his interest in the beauty-and-beast archetype, of the girl-child surrounded by monsters, some of them amiable like Kit, others sinister like Quilp. Little Nell descends to this grotesque world and then rejoins the angels; the other heroines marry into the congenial society. The girl-child among grotesques recurs in Florence Dombey's protection by Captain Cuttle, in Little Dorrit's mothering of Maggie, and in many similar scenes. Sometimes an amiable grotesque, Toots or Kit or Smike or Chivery, will attach himself to such a girl-child figure, not good enough to marry her but protesting eternal devotion nonetheless, a kind of late farcical vestige of the Courtly Love convention. Nobody turns up in *The Old Curiosity Shop* good enough to marry Little Nell, which is doubtless one reason why she dies. We may also notice the role of the old curiosity shop itself: it plays little part in the story, but is a kind of threshold symbol of the entrance into the grotesque world, like the rabbit-hole and mirror in the Alice books. Its counterparts appear in the Wooden Midshipman shop in *Dombey and Son,* the Peggotty cottage in *David Copperfield,* the bone-shop of Venus in *Our Mutual Friend,* and elsewhere.

Many of the traditional features of romantic New Comedy reached their highest point of development in nineteenth-century Britain, making it the obvious time and place for a great genius in that form to emerge. One of these, already glanced at, is the domination of narrative genres, along with a moribund drama. Dickens had many dramatic interests, but his genius was for serial romance and not for the stage. Another is the Victorian assumption of moral standards shared between author and reader. This feature makes for melodrama, where the reader emotionally participates in the moral conflict of hero and villain, or of virtue and temptation. The rigidity, or assumed rigidity, of Victorian sexual mores is a great help to a nineteenth-century plot, as it enables an author, not only to make a Wagnerian noise about a woman's extramarital escapade, but to make the most frenzied activity on her part plausible as an effort to conceal the results of it. But the relation of melodrama to the foreground action is far more important than this.

A realistic writer in the New Comedy tradition tends to work out his action on one plane: young and old, hero and humor, struggle for power within the same social group. The more romantic the writer, the more he tends to set over against his humorous world another kind of world, with which the romantic side of his story is associated. In a paper presented to the English Institute nearly twenty years ago, I spoke of the action of romantic Shakespearean comedy as divided between a foreground world of humors and a background "green world," associated with magic, sleep and dreams, and enchanted forests or houses, from which the comic resolution comes. Dickens has no green world, except for a glint or two here and there (e.g., the pastoral retreats in which Smike and Little Nell end their days, Jenny Wren's paradisal dreams, the "beanstalk" abode of Tartar in *Edwin Drood,* and the like), but he does have his own way of dividing his action. I have spoken of the nineteenth-century emphasis on the presentable, on the world of public appearance to which the nineteenth-century novelist is almost entirely confined. Behind this world lies a vast secret world, the world of privacy, where there is little or no communication. For Dickens this world is associated mainly with dreams, memories, and death. He describes it very eloquently at the opening of the third "Quarter" of *The Chimes,* and again in the first paragraph of the third chapter of *A Tale of Two Cities,* besides referring frequently to it throughout his work.

Few can read Dickens without catching the infection of his intense curiosity about the life that lies in the dark houses behind the lights of his loved and hated London. We recognize it even at second hand: when Dylan Thomas's *Under Milk Wood* opens on a night of private dreams we can see an unmistakably Dickensian influence. For most of the ironic fiction of the twentieth century, this secret world is essentially the bedroom and bathroom world of ordinary privacy, as well as the world of sexual drives, perversions, repressions, and infantile fixations that not only complements the public world but conditions one's behavior in it at every point. Characters in twentieth-century fiction have no privacy: there is no distinction between dressing-room and stage. Dickens is by no means unaware of the importance of this aspect of the hidden world, but it is of little use to him as a novelist, and he shows no restiveness about being obliged to exclude it. This is because he is not primarily an ironic writer, like Joyce or Flaubert. What he is really curious about is a hidden world of *romantic* interest, not a world even more squalid and commonplace than the visible one. His detective interest in hidden life is comparable to other aspects of Victorian culture: one thinks of the pre-Raphaelite paintings where we are challenged to guess what kind of story is being told by the picture and its enigmatic title, or of all the poems of Browning that appeal to us to deduce the reality hidden behind what is presented.

In following the main action of a Dickens novel we are frequently aware of a second form of experience being held up to it like a mirror. Sometimes this is explicitly the world of the stage. The kind of entertainment afforded by the Vincent Crummles troop in *Nicholas Nickleby* parallels the uninhibited melodrama of the main story: the dance of the savage and the

Infant Phenomenon, in particular, mirrors the Dickensian theme of the girl-child in the monster-world. In *Hard Times,* where the relation is one of contrast, a circus company symbolizes an approach to experience that Gradgrind has missed out on. The Punch and Judy show in *The Old Curiosity Shop,* one of several popular dramatic entertainments in that book, has been mentioned, and in *Great Expectations* Pip, haunted by the ghost of a father, goes to see Mr. Wopsle in *Hamlet.* Then again, Dickens makes considerable use of the curious convention in New Comedy of the doubled character, who is often literally a twin. In *The Comedy of Errors* the foreground Ephesus and the background Syracuse, in *Twelfth Night* the melancholy courts of Orsino and Olivia, are brought into alignment by twins. Similarly, the foreground action of *Little Dorrit* is related to the background action partly through the concealed twin brother of Flintwinch. In *A Tale of Two Cities,* where the twin theme is at its most complicated, the resemblance of Darnay and Carton brings the two cities themselves into alignment. In *Dombey and Son* the purse-proud world of Dombey and the other social world that it tries to ignore are aligned by the parallel, explicitly alluded to, between Edith Dombey and Alice Brown. There are many other forms of doubling, both of characters and of action, that I have no space here to examine.

The basis for such a dividing of the action might be generalized as follows. There is a hidden and private world of dream and death, out of which all the energy of human life comes. The primary manifestation of this world, in experience, is in acts of destructive violence and passion. It is the source of war, cruelty, arrogance, lust, and grinding the faces of the poor.

It produces the haughty lady with her guilty secret, like Lady Dedlock or Edith Dombey or Mrs. Clennam, the lynching mobs that hunt Bill Sikes to death or proclaim the charity of the Protestant religion in *Barnaby Rudge,* the flogging schoolmasters and the hanging judges. It also produces the courage to fight against these things, and the instinctive virtue that repudiates them. In short, the hidden world expresses itself most directly in melodramatic action and rhetoric. It is not so much better or worse than the ordinary world of experience, as a world in which good and evil appear as much stronger and less disguised forces. We may protest that its moods are exaggerated, its actions unlikely, its rhetoric stilted and unconvincing. But if it were not there nothing else in Dickens would be there. We notice that the mainspring of melodramatic action is, like that of humorous action, mainly obsession. We notice too that Dickens's hair-raising descriptions, like that of Marseilles at the opening of *Little Dorrit* with its repetition of "stare," are based on the same kind of associative rhetoric as the speech of the humors.

From this point of view we can look at the foreground action of the humors in a new light. Humors are, so to speak, petrified by-products of the kind of energy that melodrama expresses more directly. Even the most contemptible humors, the miserly Fledgeby or the hypocritical Heep, are exuberantly miserly and hypocritical: their vices express an energy that possesses them because they cannot possess it. The world they operate in, so far as it is a peaceable and law-abiding world, is a world of very imperfectly suppressed violence. They never escape from the shadow of a power which is at once Eros and Thanatos, and are bound to a passion that is never satisfied by its rationalized objects, but is ultimately self-destructive. In the earlier novels the emotional focus of this self-destroying passion is usually a miser, or a person in some way obsessed with money, like Ralph Nickleby, Dombey, Little Nell's grandfather, or Jonas Chuzzlewit. The folktale association of money and excrement, which points to the psychological origin of miserliness, appears in the "Golden Dustman" theme of *Our Mutual Friend,* and is perhaps echoed in the names Murdstone and Merdle. In the later novels a more explicitly erotic drive gives us the victim-villain figures of Bradley Headstone and Jasper Drood. Food and animals are other images that Dickens often uses in sexual contexts, especially when a miser aspires to a heroine. Arthur Gride in *Nicholas Nickleby* speaks of Madeline Bray as a tasty morsel, and Uriah Heep is compared to a whole zoo of unpleasant animals: the effect is to give an Andromeda pattern to the heroine's situation, and suggest a demonic ferocity behind the domestic foreground. The same principle of construction causes the stock-response humors like Podsnap or Gradgrind to take on a peculiar importance. They represent the fact that an entire society can become mechanized like a humor, or fossilized into its institutions. This could happen to Victorian England, according to *Hard Times,* if it takes the gospel of facts and statistics too literally, and did happen to prerevolutionary France, as described in *A Tale of Two Cities,* dying of what Dickens calls "the leprosy of unreality," and awaiting the melodramatic deluge of the Revolution.

The obstructing humors cannot escape from the ritual habits that they have set up to deal with this disconcerting energy that has turned them into mechanical puppets. The heroes and heroines, however, along with some of the more amiable humors, have the power to plunge into the hidden world of dreams and death, and, though narrowly escaping death in the process, gain from it a renewed life and energy. Sometimes this plunge into the hidden world is symbolized by a distant voyage. The incredible Australia that makes a magistrate out of Wilkins Micawber also enables the hunted convict Magwitch to become an ambiguous but ultimately genuine fairy godfather. Walter Gay in *Dombey and Son* returns from the West Indies, remarkably silent, long after he has been given up for dead, and the reader follows Martin Chuzzlewit into a place, ironically called Eden, where he is confidently expected to die and nearly does die, but where he goes through a metamorphosis of character that fits him for the comic conclusion. Other characters, including Dick Swiveller, Pip, and Esther Summerson, go into a delirious illness with the same result. *Our Mutual Friend* has a complex pattern of resurrection imagery connected with dredging the Thames, reviving from drowning, finding treasure buried in dust-heaps, and the like; a similar pattern of digging up the dead in *A Tale of Two Cities* extends from the stately Dr. Manette to the grotesque Jerry Cruncher. We notice too that the sinister society is often introduced in a kind of wavering light between sleep and waking: the appearance of the faces of Fagin and Monks at Oliver Twist's window and the alleged dreams of Abbie Flintwinch in *Little Dorrit* are examples. The most uninhibited treatment of this plunge into the world of death and dreams occurs, as we should expect, in the Christmas Books, where Scrooge and Trotty Veck see in vision a tragic version of their own lives, and one which includes their own deaths, then wake up to renewed festivity. It seems clear that the hidden world, though most of its more direct expressions are destructive and terrible, contains within itself an irresistible power of renewing life.

The hidden world is thus, once again in literature, the world of an invincible Eros, the power strong enough to force a happy ending on the story in defiance of all probability, pushing all the obstructing humors out of the way, or killing them if they will not get out of the way, getting the attractive young people disentangled from their brothers and sisters and headed for the right beds. It dissolves all hardening social institutions and reconstitutes society on its sexual basis of the family, the shadowy old fathers and mothers being replaced by new and livelier successors. When a sympathetic character dies, a strongly religious projection of this power often appears: the "Judgment" expected shortly by Miss Flite in *Bleak House,* for instance, stands in apocalyptic contrast to the Chancery court. Dickens's Eros world is, above all, a designing and manipulating power. The obstructing humor can do only what his humor makes him do, and toward the end of the story he becomes the helpless pawn of a chess game in which black can never ultimately win.

The victorious hidden world is not the world of nature in the Rousseauistic context of that word. The people who talk about this kind of nature in Dickens are such people as Mrs. Merdle in *Little Dorrit,* Mrs. Chick in *Dombey and Son,* and Wackford Squeers—not an encouraging lot. Like most romancers, Dickens gives a prominent place to the fool or "natural"—Smike, Mr. Dick, Barnaby Rudge—whose instincts make up for retarded intelligence. But such people are privileged: elsewhere nature and *social* education, or human experience, are always associated. To say that Dora Copperfield is an unspoiled child of nature is also to say that she is a spoiled child. Dickens's nature is a human nature which is the same kind of thing as the power that creates art, a designing and shaping power. This is also true of Shakespeare's green world, but Dickens's Eros world is not the conserving force that the green world is, which revitalizes a society without altering its structure. At the end of a Shakespeare comedy there is usually a figure of authority, like Prospero or the various dukes, who represents this social conservation. We have nothing in Dickens to correspond to such figures: the nearest to them are the empty Santa Claus masks of the Cheerybles, Boffin, and the reformed Scrooge. For all its domestic and sentimental Victorian setting, there is a revolutionary and subversive, almost a nihilistic, quality in Dickens's melodrama that is post-Romantic, has inherited the experience of the French Revolution, and looks forward to the world of Freud, Marx, and the existential thriller.

I used the word "absurd" earlier about Dickens's melodramatic plots, suggesting that they were creatively and not incompetently absurd. In our day the word "absurd" usually refers to the absence of purpose or meaning in life and experience, the so-called metaphysical absurd. But for literary criticism the formulating of the theory of the absurd should not be left entirely to disillusioned theologians. In literature it is design, the forming and shaping power, that is absurd. Real life does not start or stop; it never ties up loose ends; it never manifests meaning or purpose except by blind accident; it is never comic or tragic, ironic or romantic, or anything else that has a shape.

Whatever gives form and pattern to fiction, whatever technical skill keeps us turning the pages to get to the end, is absurd, and contradicts our sense of reality. The great Victorian realists subordinate their storytelling skill to their representational skill. Theirs is a dignified, leisurely vehicle that gives us time to look at the scenery. They have formed our stock responses to fiction, so that even when traveling at the much higher speed of drama, romance, or epic we still keep trying to focus our eyes on the incidental and transient. Most of us feel that there is something else in Dickens, something elemental, yet unconnected with either realistic clarity or philosophical profundity. What it is connected with is a kind of story that fully gratifies the hope expressed, according to Lewis Carroll, by the original of Alice, that "there will be nonsense in it." The silliest character in *Nicholas Nickleby* is the hero's mother, a romancer who keeps dreaming of impossible happy endings for her children. But the story itself follows her specifications and not those of the sensible people. The obstructing humors in Dickens are absurd because they have overdesigned their lives. But the kind of design that they parody is produced by another kind of energy, and one which insists, absurdly and yet irresistibly, that what is must never take final precedence over what ought to be.

Francis Russell Hart

THE EXPERIENCE OF CHARACTER IN THE

ENGLISH GOTHIC NOVEL

TWO TRENDS in the Newest Criticism of the English novel move in widely divergent directions. On one path, the numerous new apologists for romance carry forward their accrediting of prose romance as a serious post-Enlightenment genre. Theorists of American fiction lead the way. The overhaul of nineteenth-century British fiction found its momentum when Northrop Frye began reclaiming ambiguous "romance" master-pieces from the rigid "realisms" of novelistic critics. The effect has been beneficial, but extreme, and unhistorical. With each new study, it seems, more eccentric "realists" are transformed into serious romancers. Edwin M. Eigner's recent study of Stevenson gives us a Great Tradition of "serious romance" whose inclusiveness might startle Professor Frye, and certainly would puzzle some "romancers" who considered themselves "novelists" as well.[1]

[1] Edwin M. Eigner, *Robert Louis Stevenson and Romantic Tradition* (Princeton, 1966). For example, Eigner (p. 5) includes Meredith, whereas Frye (*Anatomy of Criticism* [Princeton, 1957], p. 304) cites *The Egoist* as "closer to being a typical novel." And Frye would surely be startled by Eigner's ill-informed con-clusion (p. 5) that "the serious romance in England has little to do with Scott."

Dickens has long since been relocated as a symbolic fabulist (there are, of course, welcome correctives). The old split in Scott between good novelist and bad romancer is increasingly suspect. We attend, properly, to romance motifs in the novels of Trollope and Meredith, Eliot and Hardy; we even note persistent romance affinities in the realism of Jane Austen.[2] One implication is clear. We had best stop piecemeal distinctions and concede that the old "realistic novel" was never the simple mimetic thing we once thought it, or perhaps we are just recovering from too narrow conceptions of mimesis. There have been not two distinct traditions but an ambiguous *one,* oscillating between sociological mimesis on the one hand and psychological exploration on the other. And we had best recognize that the most deliberate of "new romancers" kept an ambiguous but strong commitment to the mimetic norms of the Enlightenment novel, especially to the norm of Nature in character.

The second trend is an overdue Return to Character or characterology as an essential component of fictional mimesis. Levels and conceptions of character were, of course, emphasized in Frye's *Anatomy.* Since then have come not just important chapters on shifting characterologies (by Langbaum, Scholes, and Kellogg, for instance),[3] but numerous books: John Bayley's

[2] In *Jane Austen: A Study of Her Artistic Development* (New York, 1965), A. Walton Litz shows persuasively that Jane Austen's burlesque and parody of Gothic sentimentalism "are not necessarily acts of rejection, and if they are then the rejection is likely to be of something within the writer's own nature" (p. 14). Her "latent affinities with the 'landscape' fiction of Mrs. Radcliffe" are also noted (p. 36).

[3] Robert W. Langbaum, *The Poetry of Experience* (New York, 1963), especially Chap. V; Robert E. Scholes and Robert L. Kellogg, *The Nature of Narrative* (New York, 1966), Chaps. IV and V.

The Characters of Love, William J. Harvey's *Character and the Novel,* Charles C. Walcutt's *Man's Changing Mask.* Harvey's appendices—"The Retreat from Character" and "The Attack on Character"—conveniently summarize "the reasons why the concept of character has fallen into disrepute." [4] His book goes far toward its rehabilitation, broadening Bayley's argument that a failure of credence in character as independent existence may lead to a failure of essential understanding. The mythic critic's reduction of character to force or principle, the rhetorical critic's reduction of character to function, the stylistic critic's reduction of character to image—all obscure the very nature of meaning in traditional mimetic fiction. Such is the premise of the Return to Character, and this paper sets out to support that premise against some tendencies among the new apologists for romance. It offers no general argument. Rather, it lends its support by carrying the Return to Character into the very prototypes of post-Enlightenment romance, fictional works whose "romance" elements clearly belong to the world of novelistic norms.

Few will argue with Andrew Wright's claim that "an understanding of the literature of the last two hundred years requires a knowledge of the nature of Gothic." [5] Of late, that nature has been variously defined. [6] Gothic is a fiction evocative of

[4] *Character and the Novel* (Ithaca, N.Y., 1965), p. 192. For a different diagnosis, see Charles C. Walcutt, *Man's Changing Mask* (Minneapolis, 1966), which raises the same question, however: "Why is the criticism of fiction forever dealing with structure, values, point of view, social and psychological implications— all of which relate to character—without coming firmly to grips with the question of what *is* character exactly and how exactly is it formulated, depicted, developed in a novel?" (p. 5)

[5] *The Castle of Otranto, the Mysteries of Udolpho, Northanger Abbey* (New York, 1963), p. viii.

[6] The following summary could not be adequately documented. See especially, in addition to Montague Summers and Edith Birkhead, Michael Sadleir, *The North-*

a sublime and picturesque landscape, of an animated nature to which man is related with affective intensity. Gothic fiction is a fascination with time, with the dark persistence of the past in sublime ruin, haunted relic, and hereditary curse. The cult of ruin in Gothic, suggested Michael Sadleir, projected a symbolic bond between ruined house and nobly ruined mind. Gothic depicted a *world* in ruins, said the Divine Marquis, a world wracked by revolutionary fervor and guilt. Seen from our perspective, the Gothic signals a counter-enlightenment, climaxing an era naïve in the fervor of its scientific naturalism, its rationalism, its benevolism, its commitment to the norms of "common sense." The Gothic novelist, still "enlightened" but imperfect in his skepticism, gave to fiction a post-Enlightenment preoccupation with the preternatural, the irrational, the primordial, the abnormal, and (tending to include the rest) the demonic. It was the "historical office" of Gothic, wrote Robert Heilman, to rehabilitate the "extra-rational," to "enlarge the sense of reality and its impact on the human being." [7] It could not do so by rejecting, it did so rather by adopting and complicating, the Enlightenment's most representative literary invention, the novel.

The shocking enlargement Heilman describes is dramatized repeatedly in very different works. Ann Radcliffe's Emily, in

---

anger Novels (Eng. Assoc. Pamphlet No. 68, Oxford, 1927); Leslie Fiedler, *Love and Death in the American Novel* (New York, 1966), Chap. VI; Walter Allen, *The English Novel* (London, 1954), pp. 93–94; W. F. Axton's introduction to *Melmoth the Wanderer* (Lincoln, Neb., 1961); Angus Fletcher's interpretations of eighteenth-century Gothicism in *Allegory* (Ithaca, N.Y., 1964); Wylie Sypher, *Rococo to Cubism in Art and Literature* (New York, 1960), pp. 107–9; and (with apologies for oversights) emphatically, R. B. Heilman, "Charlotte Brontë's 'New' Gothic," reprinted in *Victorian Literature,* ed. Austin Wright (New York, 1961).

[7] Heilman, "Charlotte Brontë's 'New' Gothic," pp. 75, 84, and *passim*.

The Mysteries of Udolpho, is an enlightened heroine, a paragon of sense and sensibility. She is drawn into a world of darkness—of irrational disorder and amoral energies—and her very sense of reality is violated: "Her present life appeared like the dream of a distempered imagination, or like one of those frightful fictions in which the wild genius of the poets sometimes delighted." [8] In Lewis's *The Monk,* "Don Alphonso" and his beloved Agnes scoff at the legend of the Bleeding Nun, and at those with "a natural turn for the marvelous":

> "And you believe this, Agnes?"
>
> "How can you ask such a question? No, no, Alphonso! I have too much reason to lament superstition's influence to be its victim myself." [9]

Very enlightened, they conspire. Agnes will elope in the guise of the bloody phantom. The night comes—and Don Alphonso finds that he has carried off the phantom itself. Or recall young Catherine confronted by Heathcliff's dark malevolence, "deeply impressed and shocked at this new view of human nature." [10] Caleb Williams discovers his noble, beloved master is a secret murderer, and discovers himself:

> I felt as if my animal system had undergone a total revolution. My blood boiled within me. I was conscious to a kind

---

[8] *The Mysteries of Udolpho,* 2 vols. (London, 1931), I, 301; cf. II, 77: "So romantic and improbable, indeed, did her present situation appear to Emily herself . . . ," and elsewhere. The shock of finding one's "modern enlightened" self abruptly amid the anachronistic terrors of romance is the Radcliffian "topos" of which Scott made his "serious romance."

[9] *The Monk* (New York, 1952), pp. 152, 154.

[10] *Wuthering Heights* (Boston, 1956), p. 190.

of rapture for which I could not account . . . I was never
so perfectly alive as at that moment. . . . I felt, what I had
no previous conception of, that it was possible to love a
murderer.[11]

The dreadful, sublime shock to one's complacently enlightened
idea of human character and the reality to which it belongs—
such is the experience dramatized in Gothic fiction. It is as Heilman says. That experience is the central concern of what Eigner
calls "serious romance": "an answer to the skeptical optimism of
the perfectabilitarians." [12] It is the reflection in fiction of the
counter-enlightenment premise John Stuart Mill located in the
Germano-Coleridgians: the Enlightenment had erred from a
totally inadequate conception of human nature.[13]

Far from quarreling with such a view of the nature of
Gothic I am confirming it; it is true of old Gothic and "new
romance." My point is that what *we* mean by "romance" repudiates the novel in a way the Gothic "new romancers" never intended. When we surrender the Gothic novel to the new apologists for romance, we obscure this "nature of Gothic," whose
expression depends on the persistence of a novelistic norm of
character. But this is what the new apologists will not allow.

Northrop Frye prefaced a recent English Institute Annual
with the observation that Romanticism was inimical to the
novel, that its "contribution to prose fiction is rather, appropri-
ately enough, a form of romance." His distinction focused on

---

[11] *Caleb Williams* (New York, 1960), p. 150.

[12] *Robert Louis Stevenson,* pp. 23, 142.

[13] Cf. the essays on Bentham and Coleridge.

character: "in the romance the characters tend to become psychological projections," a restatement of the oft-quoted passage in the *Anatomy:* "the essential difference between novel and romance lies in the conception of characterization. The romancer does not attempt to create 'real people' so much as stylized figures which expand into psychological archetypes." [14] In *The Nature of Narrative,* Kellogg and Scholes subject this distinction to complex enlargement. "Characters," they concede, "are the primary vehicles for meaning in narrative." Romance (they agree with Frye) is always tending to allegory; and in allegorical romance, character does not represent—is not mimetic—is, rather, illustrative. Confronted with a mimetic character, says Kellogg, "we are justified in asking questions about his motivation based on our knowledge of the ways in which real people are motivated." With "illustrative" characters we have no right to impose such a norm, or expect such explanation: "illustrative characters are concepts in anthropoid shape or fragments of the human psyche masquerading as whole human beings." [15] This "masquerade" is precisely what some find in Gothic fiction.[16]

Scholes and Kellogg recognize that occasionally fictional characters oscillate between the mimetic (or representational)

[14] *Romanticism Reconsidered* (New York, 1963), p. 11; *Anatomy of Criticism,* p. 304.

[15] *The Nature of Narrative,* pp. 87–88, 99, 104.

[16] Cf. Eigner, *Robert Louis Stevenson,* pp. 29–39 and elsewhere. "Characters" as "doubles" are only "half-men"; Stevenson admits he is a psychologist, is ashamed of it, yet suffers (says Eigner) from thinness of characterization. After the example of Fiedler on *The Master of Ballantrae,* Eigner seems excessively inclined to read the "secret sharers" of Conrad back into the simpler central boy-rogue relationships of Stevenson.

and symbolic (or illustrative). Hawthorne they cite as a case in point. In Hawthorne's so-called "romances" a character may shift between the symbolic and the psychologically mimetic; at times we seek fullness of symbolic meaning, while at others we expect fullness of psychological explanation. The "power and intellectual complexity" of Hawthorne's fiction, they suggest, "is derived from an intricate process of oscillation." [17] There is a possibility that such distinctions of meaning and being violate the very basis of Romantic symbology, as expressed in Coleridge's insistence that a symbol must partake of its constitutive reality, must *be* in order to *mean*. Moreover, the distinctions of "level" or the discrete orders of being assumed in traditional allegory no longer obtain in a milieu of Carlyle's Natural Supernaturalism, where the symbolist conceives of "one life within us and abroad," or where the Fact is symbol. [18] But for our purposes, the idea of Hawthornian oscillation is suggestive enough in itself.

It perhaps overlooks an essential theme in Hawthorne. When a mimetic character in Hawthorne assumes symbolic dimension, that assumption is a significant fictional event. That character has, in terms of the general experience of characters *in* the fiction, deviated from the norm of character. What occurs, to

[17] *The Nature of Narrative,* p. 89.

[18] A mere passing reflection, this must be left for scrutiny elsewhere. But I wonder if its neglect vitiates Professor Fletcher's admittedly "non-historical analysis" in *Allegory;* that is, I wonder if post-Enlightenment allegory does not require careful distinction from the earlier mode. Cf. Fletcher, *Allegory,* p. 49, where the increased "possession" of Malbecco is said to effect an "intensification of the allegory," an aesthetic idea of dubious relevance to Renaissance allegory. My allusions in the text, of course, are to Coleridge, *A Statesman's Manual* and "The Eolian Harp," to Book III, Chapter 8, of *Sartor Resartus,* and to the use of "Fact" throughout *Past and Present.*

apply Angus Fletcher's analogy,[19] is a form of demonic possession; this is NOT the same thing (*pace* Fletcher) that happens
to Despair or Malbecco in *The Faerie Queene,* who change
from personification to symbol, but not from mimetic character
to demonic emblem. In Hawthorne, life has become allegory.
Romantic allegory is not a rhetorical mode but a representation
of reality transformed by the intervention of a new significance
of being. The chief problem of Hawthorne's characters becomes
the problem of how to react to the demonic typology thrust
upon them, or—like Yeats's Magi—to the terror of incarnation.
It is not normal in the world of Blithesdale or the Easter Rising
for human personality abruptly to assume typological or sacra-
mental force, any more than it is "natural" for characters in
Gothic novels to find themselves thrust into a world of "romance." The shock is theirs. The mystery is the experience
which they, in their humanity as characters, must cope with. To
do so, they must exist for the reader basically as mimetic characters, characters to be understood in terms of psychological probability and process.

And this is what the apologists for romance would have
them *not* do. For they would have them belong to a narrative
mode where such representational being is an excrescence, an
authorial mistake. Such is Leslie Fiedler's position. In the history
of the novel, he says, we have "two modes, analytic and projective." In one we expect "fully motivated characters in the analytic sense"; in the other we find "mere projections of uncon-

---

[19] Chapter I ("The Daemonic Agent") of *Allegory* rests on the analogy—the near
identification—of rhetorical distortion of character and monomaniacal distortion
of personality.

scious guilt or fear . . . simple projection[s] with an inner logic
rather than a psychology." Gothic novels, we shall see, are
crammed with psychological exposition; but this, in Fiedler's
view, is a *mistake*—

> a confusion at the heart of the gothic about its own method
> and meaning. Precisely because the early practitioners of the
> tale of terror were only half aware of the symbolic nature of
> their genre, they did not know what kind of credence to ask
> for their protagonists—presenting them sometimes as fully
> motivated characters in the analytic sense, and at others, as
> mere projections of unconscious guilt or fear— [20]

that is, characters with no psychology, with no independent
representational existence. If only we allow ourselves this reduc-
tive teleology, we are free to overlook all the complex psychologizing and read character as projection or archetype. Heathcliff
can then be a spiritual force or principle, and Rochester the fig-
ment of a girl's erotic fancy. Melmoth not only suspects he is,
but *is* Cain or Ahasuerus incarnate; and the monster of that
modern Prometheus Frankenstein *is* the demonic projection of
his creator's fallen mind. Godwin's Falkland *is* Divine Pursuer,
Hound of Heaven. Lewis's Monk, like the hero-villains of Ann
Radcliffe, is the archetypal Shadow, the dark side of the psyche,
pursuing the passive anima. And they all live together on a
nightmare landscape, in a subjective visionary world, where such
things (says Fiedler) can happen.[21]

The trouble with such readings is not that they are untrue

[20] *Love and Death in the American Novel,* p. 141.
[21] *Ibid.,* p. 140.

but that the sense in which they *are* true is misrepresented so as to obscure the question raised by the novels. Consider the question in some of its most famous manifestations. It haunts all of Heathcliff's victims in *Wuthering Heights*. "That incarnate goblin!—Monster!" says his wife. "Hush, hush! He's a human being," replies Nelly Dean. "He's not a human being," insists Mrs. Heathcliff; and Nelly wonders:

"Is he a ghoul, or a vampire?" I mused. I had read of such hideous, incarnate demons. And then, I set myself to reflect, how I had tended him in infancy; and watched him grow to youth; and followed him almost through his whole course; and what absurd nonsense it was to yield to that sense of horror.

"But, where did he come from, the little dark thing, harboured by a good man to his bane?" muttered superstition, as I dozed into unconsciousness.[22]

Heathcliff asks the same question about Cathy: human being or demon? Are the old superstitions true, after all? "Are you possessed with a devil?" he shouts. Is this a world of nature, or do we find our enlightened selves face to face with the preternatural, in shapes we had *thought* were human?

When first they meet in the forest, Jane Eyre and Edward Rochester suspect each other of being demons. As Rochester's horse approaches, Jane's enlightenment deserts her:

In those days I was young, and all sorts of fancies bright and dark tenanted my mind: the memories of nursery sto-

[22] *Wuthering Heights,* pp. 147, 280.

ries were there amongst other rubbish. . . . As this horse approached, and as I watched for it to appear through the dusk, I remembered certain of Bessie's tales, wherein figured a North-of-England spirit, called a "Gytrash." [23]

Rochester recalls the meeting in reverse; for him, Jane was the demon.

"When you came upon me in Hay Lane last night, I thought unaccountably of fairy tales, and had half a mind to demand whether you had bewitched my horse: I am not sure yet. . . . And so you were waiting for your people when you sat on that stile? . . . For the men in green."

Neither is quite of the societal world. Jane the child had been strange; her aunt, we are told, "really did not know whether I were child or fiend." Locked in the haunted room, Jane looks in the mirror and sees that the haunt is herself:

All looked colder and darker in that visionary hollow than in reality; and the strange little figure there gazing at me, with a white face and arms specking the gloom, and glittering eyes of fear moving where all else was still, had the effect of a real spirit: I thought it like one of the tiny phantoms, half fairy, half imp, Bessie's evening stories represented as coming up out of lone, ferny dells in moors.

The experience of the enlightened person feeling haunted by some demonic self: this is the center of the fiction. What manner of being is this?

[23] *Jane Eyre* (Boston, 1959), p. 108. The following quotations from *Jane Eyre* are from pp. 117–18 and 14.

In a very different novel of ambiguous demonology, *Frankenstein,* the student of nature becomes obsessed with the creation of life and makes a man. Horrified with what he has done he sees it as a demon. Is it? Or is it just a hideous man? Is it a devilish conjuration of Frankenstein's mind, or has it its own human nature? According to the monster, it has, and he traces the course of that nature: needing love and society, suffering from his creator's rejection, he appeals everywhere. No one will accept or respond to his humanity. Frankenstein assures us that the monster's plea is hellishly untrue, the lie of a demon. Whom do we believe? What manner of being is this?

In *Caleb Williams* everyone feels haunted by a demon in everyone else.[24] The persecuted Emily, like her sister heroines in Radcliffe and Lewis, feels her pursuer Tyrrel to be a "devil incarnate." Tyrrel suffers "the torment of demons" because he is haunted by Falkland: "That man is a legion of devils to me!" But for Falkland, Tyrrel "seemed to realize all that had been told of the passions of fiends," and his effect on Falkland's life is "the pestilential influence of some demon." The pestilence spreads until Falkland becomes the pursuing demon of Caleb; at the climax, the roles are reversed and Caleb feels himself the demon who has destroyed Falkland.

The central question persists in Maturin's *Melmoth the Wanderer.* This seemingly immortal wanderer who offers earthly sufferers release in return for their souls—is he demon or man? is he really different from other men? The prisoner Stanton, the victim of avaricious relatives, accosts his tempter with "You, demon!" Melmoth's answer is a recurrent theme: "De-

[24] *Caleb Williams,* pp. 23, 35, 61, 75, 93, 97, 139.

mon!—Harsh words!—Was it a demon or a human being
placed you here?"[25] Other sufferers in the book are thrilled
with the horrible suspicion that they are tormented by demons;
Melmoth wrestles with the knowledge that he is *possessed* by
one—a "demon of superhuman misanthropy"—and counters
with the terrible possibility that all men are—or can be—agents
of the devil, demonic at their most noble, demonic for those they
love most.

The novelist deals, we are told, with *social* man. In Hillis
Miller's terms, it was the form invented to explore the various
forms interpersonal relations may take. In all of these novels the
question of the demonic in nature is referred to *social* relationship. The demonic is virtually a function of relationship: as in
Blake's seminal Romantic myth of "spectres" and "emanations,"
characters haunt and pursue each other in demonic malevolence
when normal unities disintegrate or relations are thwarted. Love
thwarted becomes destructive; lovers live only to pursue each
other in possessive fury. Brontesque lovers torment each other
demonically, until—if ever—the mutual love of separate, whole
existences becomes possible. Frankenstein's creation seems "my
own vampire, my own spirit let loose from the grave, and forced
to destroy all that was dear to me." But his creation has *become*
this way because social love has been denied him: "My heart
was fashioned to be susceptible of love and sympathy; and when
wrenched by misery to vice and hatred it did not endure the violence of the change without torture such as you cannot even
imagine." It is no devilish sophistry that causes the monster's
"exclamation of grief and horror" over Frankenstein's body. The

[25] *Melmoth the Wanderer*, p. 42.

last appeal is the monster's; the final authenticity of his human pathos, his human isolation, is undeniable: the enemy of God "had friends and associates in his desolation; I am alone." [26] No mythic reading of the monster as spectre, spawned and spurned by Frankenstein's "distorted psychological energies," [27] provides for this essentially novelistic image of character socially persecuted and rejected. Likewise, the characters in *Caleb Williams* are naturally social beings who assume demonic roles in relation to each other. Each has his autonomous and explicable nature; each becomes a demonic spectre or projection *only* as a result of the perversion of social love; each has a nature distinct from that demonic role. If the novel is reduced to parable or to myth—the parable of the soul wrestling with an angry God; the myth of psychological doubles, secret sharers [28]—then this essential duplicity is lost. The demonic is no longer represented as the corruption of nature in social relationship.

The original field for human relationship in *Wuthering Heights,* as in *Frankenstein,* is social, domestic. The final image of good in *Wuthering Heights* is social marriage; for me, no other reading is true to the book's form. The same image pre-

---

[26] *Frankenstein* (New York, 1965), pp. 76, 218, 220.

[27] As in, for instance, Muriel Spark, *Child of Light* (Hadleigh, Essex, 1951), p. 137: "We may visualize Frankenstein's doppelgänger or Monster firstly as representing reason in isolation, since he is the creature of an obsessional rational effort."

[28] Allen, *The English Novel* (pp. 96–97), says it is an index of Godwin's successful use of symbol that the reader "may if he wishes see in this study of the hunter and hunted who in the end find that their enmity is really love, a profound symbolic rendering of the relation between God and man." I am not suggesting that a novel cannot be symbolic; I am suggesting that such a "reading" of *Caleb Williams* must not just overlook, but deny, the essential socio-psychological meaning of Falkland's tragedy as a character.

vails in *Jane Eyre*. No attempt at an experience of untrammeled spirit, of non-social love, is ultimately meaningful. Melmoth and his Immalee yearn in vain for some transcendent realm above the conditions of nature and society where their love can be free. But Immalee assumes the cultural identity of Isidora, and Melmoth's habitual cynicism and power-lust make it inevitable that he seek to damn her, just as Lewis's Monk, his social nature perverted, must destroy his Antonia.

Emily St. Aubert and Montoni are mysteriously related, and both have characters distinct from their roles. The heroine's destiny, working through her character, her passionate curiosity and Gothic imagination, demands that she become implicated with violence and amoral power in order to establish her heritage and realize her social identity. In the climactic image of this theme she not only consorts with ghosts, but is one; to those bound to her in guilt she is the mirror image of a murdered past, the spectre of past sin like Esther on the Ghost's Walk in *Bleak House*. She plays a demonic role in this ritual enactment, yet the role is distinct from her character. In character she must assimilate her own temporary role just as she must expand her sense of reality to accommodate the vision of the evil Montoni.

Montoni, too, has his duplicity. He can be understood in terms of social masks: he is an opportunist, an imprudent gamester, a selfish bandit. His motives, we hear, are "entirely selfish, those of avarice and pride." [29] But the Montoni of Emily's experience is no shallow social villain; for her, his chief significance is in his non-social vitality. He "delighted in the energies of the passions," an animating joy alien to the ordered

[29] *Mysteries of Udolpho*, I, 278; subsequent quotations are from I, 185, and II, 27.

world of sense and sensibility. Emily's experience of Montoni and his castle is the frightening essence of "romance." But when the experience of "romance" is complete, Montoni fades once more into the thwarted social villain.

In short, the central "love" relationship in Gothic novels is a mystery in which autonomous natural existences—characters—come to assume demonic roles. Hence, it sheds as ambiguous a light on human character as the central question we have already identified: are demons real after all? Is there a supernatural that is part of the natural world? What manner of being is this?

The answer consistently is, he is a man, and yet. . . . He is of Nature; we can understand him naturally, explain him psychologically, as a man, and yet. . . . Now if we believe that this character is not mimetic but symbolic, a concept in anthropoid shape, then the point is lost. What gives the point its full and terrifying truth in an enlightenment context is that the demonic is no myth, no superstition, but a reality in human character or relationship, a novelistic reality. Goethe, contemporary of Gothic novelists, said it thus: "This daemonic character appears in its most *dreadful* form when it stands out dominatingly in some *man.*"[30] Are there really *ghosts?* asks Carlyle-Teufelsdröckh. *We* are ghosts.

To get the point we must accept first the explicability of man as character; and in the novels I have mentioned, this is the way he accepts himself. He assumes his human reality, and

[30] Quoted from *Dichtung und Wahrheit* by Rudolph Otto, *The Idea of the Holy,* trans. J. W. Harvey (London, 1957), p. 152. Fletcher (*Allegory,* p. 40n) called my attention to the passage, but he gives no emphasis to the idea that "most *dreadful*" is daemonic *man.*

when this assumption no longer suffices, then he is as baffled as we. The novels are necessarily filled with psychological exposition, with the kind of expository intervention that distracts Fiedler, or any reader who adjusts to a character as projective or symbolic only to have it naturalistically "explained." Such a reader sees confusion where there is an intention of meaningful paradox. Heathcliff is a demonic mystery, yet, insists Nelly to herself, I watched him grow; I traced his natural "course." Rochester and Jane may be strangers to this societal world, yet their strangeness must be domesticated to the earthly destiny of characters in a novel. Falkland may seem like god or demon, yet his story is told to demonstrate that he can be naturally explained. And recall the complexity of character exposition in the most extreme of our "romances," *The Monk* and *Melmoth the Wanderer.*

Few psychological processes have been documented more fully than the gradual degradation of Lewis's Ambrosio. Any interpreter of him as a nightmare monster, a dark symbol of sexual violation, must overlook many pages of character exposition. The reader may not want them; he may reject them as bad psychology or bad fictional method; but they are there nonetheless, and they establish a norm of character. The novel ends with the assurance that the wanton Mathilda, Ambrosio's seducer, is no woman but a crafty demon in Satan's service. It is no accident that many readers find this unacceptable.[31] Mathilda has been consistently drawn as a human agent whose passion for Ambrosio progresses through natural phases. Ambrosio's own

[31] Cf. John Berryman in the introduction to *The Monk* (New York, 1952), p. 16: "It has been rightly pointed out that the Fiend's claim about Matilda's nature at the end is inconsistent with all that has gone before, a blunder of Lewis's."

"bosom" is a "theatre of a thousand contending passions." [32] We are made to attend to the psychological laws by which the warm, conscientious monk becomes the apprehensive hypocrite. We are given lengthy explanations of the process whereby nurture affixes an artificial character to his nature:

> It was by no means his nature to be timid: but his education had impressed his mind with fear so strongly, that apprehension was now become part of his character. . . . the contest for superiority between his real and acquired character was striking and unaccountable to those unacquainted with his original disposition.[33]

To Antonia and other innocents he must seem an "unaccountable" monster. To us, he is a complex natural being.

In Melmoth's case, the psychologizing is equally undeniable. For his world Melmoth has become an inscrutable being of supernatural powers, eternally roaming the earth. But his habitat is graphically localized first and last in rural Ireland; and if he is a Cain, he is a "Cain of the moral world"—we would say a Cain psychologized. He has entered the realm of myth; he has become a legendary scourge, a reality remote from human imagining, yet it is to his humanizing, his de-mythologizing, that we attend throughout. Far from seeing character transformed into symbol or myth, we see myth psychologized into explicable character. From within we see the natural humanity of Melmoth striving to liberate itself from its fated demonic role: "with all his diabolical heartlessness, he *did* feel some relentings

[32] *The Monk*, p. 103.
[33] *Ibid.*, pp. 229, 237–39.

of his human nature"; but alas! "the habitual character of his dark and fiendish pursuit, rushed back on him."[34] It is the distinction of *The Monk* over again: nature struggles with the artificial but "habitual character" affixed by his demonic role. In his full humanity, Melmoth is pathetically aware of the struggle. He marvels in horror at the "demoniacal character" he has acquired: "the world could show him no greater marvel than his own existence." But it is no marvel of a Faustian folk superstition; his diabolism, he well knows, is of another kind, and to those who look upon him with naïve superstition his enlightened answer is the book's reiterated theme. Diabolism is in every man:

> I tell you, whenever you indulged one brutal passion, one sordid desire, one impure imagination—whenever you uttered one word that wrung the heart, or embittered the spirit of your fellow creature . . . whenever you have done this, you have been ten times more an agent of the enemy of man than all the wretches whom terror, enfeebled nerves, or visionary credulity, has forced into the confession of an incredible compact with the author of evil.[35]

His demonism, he insists, is inseparable from the humanity of an explicable natural world—and we believe him because his own human torments are fully analyzed before our eyes. The "Cain," the figure of Faustian legend, is transformed into a character in a novel, and demands appropriate credence.

[34] *Melmoth the Wanderer,* pp. 229, 233, 241. One might also trace the analogous characterization of Immalee, seen first as supernatural being, then unfallen child of nature, then Isidora, long-lost daughter of a Spanish nobleman.

[35] *Ibid.,* pp. 50, 274, 334.

This is not to say that he necessarily always wins it. It is the business of critical judgment to determine the success with which, in each novel, that credence is effected. I have not meant to evaluate individual works, to assess the quality or fullness of their psychological power or truth. I have wanted only to show their common intention and thus to show the "novelistic" standard by which they must all be judged. If, in some cases, this is to argue that an "interesting romance" is in fact an inferior novel, that cannot be helped. If a book's salvation is to depend on misunderstanding and misclassification, the true ends of criticism are surely not served. And in this case, much misunderstanding obscures the real historical impulse of the Gothic novel.

Rather than representing a flight from novel to romance, the Gothic represents a naturalizing of myth and romance into novel. However the late Enlightenment theorists of fiction differed, they agreed on the primacy in "new romance"—the novel—of what we call mimetic character.[36] The demand for "characters of nature" dominates Johnson's praise of Shakespeare and his preference for Richardson among novelists. For Clara Reeve and John Moore, the "Progress of Romance" moved inevitably to the detailed rendition of "characters of nature."

[36] In his naturalizing of myth and romance the Gothic novelist seems kin to the German Romantic maker of *Kunstmärchen*, "fairy-tales in which a sophisticated artist makes use of the folklore materials and naive effects of the *Volksmärchen*, or popular fairy story, to create what was, when Goethe founded it, virtually a new genre." (Robert Wolff, *The Golden Key* [New Haven, 1961], p. 45). But the *Kunstmärchen* was "a species of writing never domesticated in English" (G. B. Tennyson, *Sartor Called Resartus* [Princeton, 1965], p. 76). This is to overlook George MacDonald and Oscar Wilde, certainly, but it may be that the "taste for the natural" proved so strong as to cause the English author to limit his naturalizing to the Protean novel.

Mme de Staël derives the novel as a Rousseauistic medium of
intricate psychological individuation; Mrs. Barbauld salutes
Richardson, "father of the modern novel," for satisfying the new
"taste for the natural." In the late Enlightenment's poetics of
fiction, the "taste for the natural" was held paramount in the
effecting of imaginative belief. Coleridge was joining a tradition
when he professed (in 1817) that the aim of his preternat-
uralism in the *Lyrical Ballads* was "the interesting of the affec-
tions by the dramatic truth of such emotions, as would naturally
accompany such situations supposing them real." There follows
as accurate a description of Gothic mimesis as one could find:
"And real in this sense they have been to every human being
who, from whatever source of delusion, has at any time believed
himself under supernatural agency." [37] It is essentially the ra-
tionale invoked by Shelley when, a year later, he wrote his wife's
preface to *Frankenstein:*

> I have not considered myself as merely weaving a series of
> supernatural terrors. . . . [However improbable, the story]
> affords a point of view to the imagination for the delineat-
> ing of human passions. . . . I have thus endeavored to pre-
> serve the truth of the elementary principles of human
> nature.

But the pioneer had set the keynote long before. However
shoddy his own adherence, Horace Walpole formulated a mimetic code for "new romance" in 1764, and established the norm
of character the Gothic novelists were to follow. His purpose, in
The Castle of Otranto, he insisted, was

[37] *Biographia Literaria,* Chap. XIV.

to conduct the mortal agents in his drama according to the rules of probability; in short, to make them think, speak and act, as it might be supposed mere men and women would do in extraordinary positions.

His model was "inspired writings," where

the personages under the dispensation of miracles and witnesses to the most stupendous phenomena, never lose sight of their human character.[38]

If we "lose sight of their human character," we shall miss their meaning.

[38] Preface to the Second Edition.

K. J. Fielding

DICKENS AND THE PAST: THE NOVELIST

OF MEMORY

EVERYONE KNOWS THE STORY of how, when Dickens was a boy, he had to work in the blacking-factory. We know it, if in no other way, through the use he made of it in the chapters about Murdstone and Grinby's in *David Copperfield.* And nearly everyone interested in Dickens will also know it from the wonderful account he gave of his childhood, parts of which (all that remain) are preserved in his *Life* by John Forster.[1] The story of his lost childhood, and how—with rare exceptions—he refused to speak about it, is as memorable as his fiction; and, as a result of this, we sometimes have later biographers than Forster bringing Dickens before us as a man who was afraid of his past, who turned away from it and suppressed it. Yet what I chiefly want to suggest, without entirely contradicting this, is that he was someone who felt dogged by his past and that, seeking to understand himself, he turned back to try to reexplore it and remake it.

So the novel I shall chiefly look at is *Little Dorrit,* with

[1] John Forster, *Life of Charles Dickens,* ed. J. W. T. Ley (London, 1928), chiefly in Book I, chap. ii, "Hard Experiences in Boyhood."

some reference to *David Copperfield* and Dickens's other writings; and, first, I simply want to recall how intense his relationship with his childhood was. I suppose that all readers of *David Copperfield* realize that it is especially a novel of memory; and I suggest that we should see that this is also true of much of Dickens's other work, especially *Little Dorrit,* which is read best by keeping this in mind. That is my main point; but, in coming to it, I want to suggest that, although a novelist's exploitation of his own life and personality was part of the tradition of the novel in which Dickens was then writing, he also came to be peculiarly concerned with it. It may even have happened that, after writing two novels as personal or autobiographical as *David Copperfield* and *Little Dorrit,* his own nature partly changed. For, as he understood himself, and withdrew into himself, more, he became less interested in the world about him—for the one was the obverse of the other. He came—perhaps—to see, in fact, that in trying to escape from himself by writing about his own society he was also expressing his own problems that had originated in childhood. Now, once he understood or believed this, although he understood himself better, he became more self-conscious and it restricted his spontaneity. And this may partly even have led to his turning to the stage to give his public readings, with that "substitution," as John Forster has it, "of lower for higher aims."

This is a suggestion, therefore, of how we may see Dickens, not a final analysis. It follows from an attempt to grasp as many of the pieces as possible in his life and writings of this middle period, and to see what pattern they make. For it seems to me there should be nothing contradictory between a novelist's writings and his life; and, if we can use one to help us understand the other, then we should.

Thus, in thinking first of Dickens's preoccupation with his own past, there are various ways in which this may be seen. We can learn it from the novels, from Dickens's miscellaneous writings, and from his biographers or those who knew him. Of the last of these, John Forster is the most remarkable, for in Forster we have the only authority on Dickens who ever discussed his childhood with him, and the only person who has written about Dickens who was informed (though he did not tell us everything) about the curious pattern of Dickens's life after 1858.

It was to Forster that Dickens first confided (in April, 1847) about his childhood, as a result of his friend's saying that Charles Dilke, the elder, claimed to remember tipping the boy Dickens a half-crown and receiving "a very low bow." As a direct consequence, Dickens wrote the first part of his autobiography and showed it to Forster (as he did to Mrs. Dickens); and, later, discussed it with him in relation to *David Copperfield*. Forster was closely consulted about the progress of the novels at this time; and although he tends also to speak of "the autobiographical form" of *Copperfield* as in the tradition of Henry Fielding (as he wrote in the *Examiner,* May 3, 1849, p. 177) and of "the early and greater masters of English fiction," he was also well aware of it as a fresh departure for Dickens and his first *major* essay in the exploration of his past. This needs to be emphasized because it had been preceded by the Christmas Book of 1848, *The Haunted Man,* which was also obviously affected by Dickens's new self-examination. For this book had given, rather too directly, the thoughts of a man who had suffered "a great wrong done him early in life"; and it had evolved the moral, as Forster explains it, that we should never seek to forget the past, since "bad and good are inextricably linked."

Of course, *David Copperfield* is much more subtle than this Christmas Book in its sense of Time and its examination of the author's self; and it is distinguished from the later novels by its self-assurance that by self-mastery a man may live down what might have harmed him. For, as Forster says, "up to the date of the completion of *Copperfield* [Dickens] felt himself to be in possession of an all-sufficient resource," sure in his art that there was a "world he could bend to his will." [2] It is only after this stage that he began to feel, like Mrs. Clennam in *Little Dorrit* confronted by the past, that "It is closing in." The direction of *Copperfield* is toward fulfillment, as when David is united with Agnes and "long miles of road then open out before his mind," and he recognizes "toiling on . . . a ragged way-worn boy, who should come to call the heart even now beating against mine, his own." The sense of *Little Dorrit* is of confinement, as when Arthur parts from Minnie and all his old hopes, and "the trees," in the avenue where they have met, "seemed to close up behind them, like their own perspective of the past."

Three recent writers comment on Dickens's growing sense of Time, especially as shown in *David Copperfield*. One is Hillis Miller (in *Charles Dickens; The World of His Novels,* 1958); the second, John Raleigh in his "Dickens and the Sense of

---

[2] *Ibid.,* Book VIII, chap. ii, "What Happened at This Time." This chapter and Book II, chap. ii, give most of what Forster has to say on Dickens and his "past."

Time" (*Nineteenth Century Fiction,* XIII [1958], 127–37);
and the third, Jerome Buckley in his *The Triumph of Time*
(1966). All of them notice how conscious Dickens is of Time
in this novel, from David's question about the memory of his
mother—"Can I say of her face . . . perished as I know it
is—that it is gone, when here it comes before me . . . as distinct
as any face that I may choose to look on?"—to his repeated
awareness of how, later on, his sense of self chiefly depends on
memory awakened by associations of words, places, people,
events, and physical sensations—as when David tells how "even
at this day [at the time of writing] the scent of a geranium leaf
strikes me with a half-comical, half-serious wonder as to what a
change has come over me," as he thus recalls the summer
afternoon he spent with Dora lingering in the garden of her
home at Norwood. It has to be agreed with them that *David
Copperfield* is Dickens's "most personal book" (Miller, p. 151)
and that it is "above all others his novel of memory" (Buckley,
p. 108).

In going on with *Bleak House* and *Hard Times,* Dickens
clearly made much more use of this sense of Time that he did
before he had so searchingly retraced his childhood. Yet these
works are less personal: for though they are concerned to show
how, through Time, our lives inevitably work toward fulfillment, they represent patterns of events more than development
through experience.

All this is common, well-trodden ground; and it is no less
undeniable, I think, that in *David Copperfield* the "mode of
memory was not difficult for Dickens" (Miller, p. 153). It came
to him easily, and yet to some extent there is also an attempt to

remake the past. For while Dickens saw himself clearly as like David in his sense of an "unhappy loss or want of something," he ends by making a break with his past and providing what he himself seems to have thought a "dangerous comfort" in the fulfillment with Agnes. In a real sense this was a denial of himself. Certainly, when we arrive at *Little Dorrit*—and the time of strain which preceded its writing and which soon led to the breakup of his home life and the pattern of his whole career—we come to a period in which his writing was hardly less personal or concerned with memory, even though it was impossible to write fiction as autobiography so directly again.

The main difference between *Copperfield* and *Little Dorrit* is surely that, in *Copperfield,* Dickens remained apparently confident in his progress from the "high rock in the ocean" of Time (ch. 9) which stood for the death of his mother, to his union with Agnes, "my love of whom was founded on a rock" (ch. 62); and we see that the only irony of his "reflections," when as an adult he revisits his childhood home, is that they were associated with "the distinguished things I was to do"—and that these are fulfilled. The novel suggests that Dickens was still satisfied (or wanted to be satisfied), as he wrote in his autobiography, to "know how all these things have worked together to make of me what I am."

Yet between the writing of *Copperfield* and *Dorrit* we know that he became "restless" and dissatisfied; and, whereas Forster ascribes this largely to a loss of spontaneity in writing (or "a certain strain upon his invention"), Dickens blamed it on "miseries of older growth . . . as with poor David, . . . a sense . . . of one happiness I have missed in life," arising from both his childhood and his marriage.[3] All biographers naturally also link it with his age, the growing-up of his children, and the incompatibility with his wife. We are clearly unable to separate causes and results; but the consequence when he came to his next novel was evidently an even greater concern with Time through the inability of its characters to escape their past.

It is, perhaps, at this point that the objection must be faced that to involve autobiography and fiction may help neither, and while that is possibly excusable with *David Copperfield,* where the text even overlaps Dickens's written autobiography, it can only be confusing with other novels. This should not be confidently and completely denied. Yet the interaction is completely true to Dickens. For Dickens had become desperately preoccupied with himself. Forster, again, reminds us: "Sterne did not more incessantly fall back from his works upon himself than Dickens did"; and he wisely remarks that "undoubtedly one of the impressions [Dickens leaves] is that of the intensity and tenacity with which he recognized, realized, contemplated, cultivated and thoroughly enjoyed, his own individuality in even its most trivial manifestations."[4] A rift was thus opening between his own nature and one of his most convinced beliefs that no one's sympathies should be enclosed within himself. It is this rift which the later novels explore.

This cult of personality on Dickens's part is abundantly obvious, and both he and Forster pointedly relate it to his childhood experiences. Both of them were also surely more aware than we sometimes give them credit for that the Novel (even as they knew it) was peculiarly adapted to expressing an author's

[3] *Ibid.,* p. 639.   [4] *Ibid.,* p. 818.

triumphant sense of individuality whether in the hands of Fielding, Sterne, or others of Forster's "early and greater masters of English fiction." To these names might be added Defoe. For though we may pass lightly over half-fanciful comparisons between *David Copperfield* and *Robinson Crusoe,* though Yarmouth was the scene of Crusoe's first shipwreck as of Steerforth's, young David is said to be "more solitary" than he, and even Aunt Betsy is likened to "a female Robinson Crusoe." Dickens does frequently remind us of his admiration for Defoe, as for example in a most significant essay, "Where We Stopped Growing" (*Household Words,* VI [January 1, 1853], 361–63).

This is somewhat fanciful; but it may suggest to us how one of the traditions of these "early masters" was that the novelist was often especially concerned with himself. For Ian Watt reminds us [5] that Defoe in particular felt himself to be, like his hero, "an isolated and solitary figure of his own time," conscious that he stood alone in the world, having "forced his way with undiscouraged diligence." As with Defoe, so it is with Dickens. There were times when even Forster is compelled to admit that Dickens was no less an egotist. Yet there was a great difference between the two novelists in that, at the same time, there was nothing in the world that Dickens was so determined to oppose in the world about him.

For Dickens's sense of irony, sensitivity, and imagination made him self-aware; and his powers of sympathy may even have arisen partly from his own sense that he stood alone, combined with his conviction that men must not isolate themselves. For, again and again, Dickens repeats the theme in his novels

[5] *The Rise of the Novel* (London, 1963), p. 93.

that to shut out the word or to dwell on the past alone is wrong. Before *Great Expectations* and Miss Havisham, for example, he had affirmed in *Little Dorrit* that "to stop the clock of busy existence, at the hour when we were personally sequestered from it; to suppose mankind stricken motionless . . . is the infirmity of many invalids, and the mental unhealthiness of many recluses" (ch. 29). Before *Little Dorrit,* in that same essay "Where We Stopped Growing," Dickens passes in a very natural transition from ways in which he fancies himself fixed in tastes and attitudes formed in childhood to the recollection of an actual Woman in White and a Woman in Black who had once been familiar figures in the London streets of Dickens's boyhood.

These figures are interesting: the real Woman in White was a Quakeress always in her bridal dress because the man she was to marry had deserted her. The Woman in Black was in perpetual mourning for her only brother—a bank clerk—who had been executed years before for forgery, but whom she passed her days inquiring for in the City. They were not characters of Dickens's invention, although they clearly helped to give rise to Miss Havisham. They did inhabit the London of his boyhood; they were even impersonated on the stage by a popular actor for a night before he was hissed off.[6] So in this essay, "Where We Stopped Growing," they are also seen as fixed in relation to their past: like the Haunted Man and Dickens, too, they have been checked by some real or imaginary wrong. Here, therefore, Dickens seems to have been partly recognizing himself. With Bounderby (a year later) he was even to be amused at the man

[6] Martin Meissel, "Miss Havisham Brought to Book," *PMLA*, LXXXI (1966), 278–85.

of achievement who disowns his parents. The time was still to come when he would write self-excusingly to Forster (in June, 1862) in reply to his friend's suggestion that he was losing his former generosity:

> I must entreat you to pause . . . and to go back to what you know of my childish days, and to ask yourself whether it is natural that something of the character formed in me then . . . should have reappeared in the last five years. The never to be forgotten misery of that old time, bred a certain shrinking sensitiveness in a certain ill-clad ill-fed child, that I have found to come back in the never to be forgotten misery of this later time.[7]

Only by that time did he come to realize that his nature had been inescapably formed by the past—even, perhaps, that it was one that he had cultivated: no less, that his sympathies as an artist and his ironies as a social critic were largely determined by it. It is this that Forster evidently recognizes when he explains Dickens's difficulties of 1855–58:

> There was for him "no city of the mind" against outward ills, for inner consolation and shelter. It was in and from the actual he still stretched forward to find the freedoms and satisfactions of an ideal and by his very attempts to escape the world he was driven back into the thick of it.[8]

The world was himself. As much as the figure in his manuscript notebook, begun at this time, he may have felt he was "The man whose vista is always stopped up by the image of

[7] Forster, *Life,* Book I, chap. iii, p. 39.   [8] *Ibid.,* p. 641.

Himself" [9]—the great difference being that Dickens was aware of it.

So, now, in many of his minor writings, and in the major novels of the last period, not only was Dickens concerned to think out his own past, but one of the major themes of the novels is how the past may affect anyone—as it affected him— and what response should be made. It was even acted out in his life. For it was not suppressed, though it *was* concealed.

There is the well-known story, for example, told by Sir Henry Fielding Dickens, of how in a Christmas Party "Memory Game," the Christmas before his death, Dickens brought out at the end of a string of triumphantly remembered words

> his own contribution, "Warren's Blacking, 30, Strand." He gave this with an odd twinkle in his eye, and a strange inflection in his voice which at once forcibly attracted my attention and left a vivid impression on my mind for some time afterwards.

Yet Henry Dickens had not then the "faintest idea" of what his father "had gone through." [10]

Dickens, in some ways, evidently enjoyed living in the past, although he would have been horrified had it been exposed. I did not notice until recently how pointedly he hints at it, for example, in the "Preface" to *Little Dorrit* written when the book was finished. For he particularly says, there, that he did not go to look at what was left of the Marshalsea until "I was approach-

[9] Dickens notebook, begun January, 1855, Berg Collection, New York Public Library.

[10] *Memories of My Father* (London, 1928), pp. 23–24.

ing the end of this story." When he did so, he went on, he saw
how the "great Block" still preserved the "rooms that arose in my
mind's-eye when I became Little Dorrit's biographer." A little
boy he met showed preternatural acuteness about "the room
where Little Dorrit was born," which he was quite "a quarter of
a century too young to know anything about . . . of himself."
So this should have left its readers asking how Dickens could
have come to know just what the inside of the Marshalsea was
like in 1826 if he had not been back to see it since the outer wall
had gone. But it is certain that, if anyone asked, no one was
told.

There is another more involved biographical sequence which,
as an example of this kind of behavior, calls for attention because of a fresh discovery. It arises out of Dickens's passionate
interest in the inquests on the deaths of over one hundred and
fifty children, on a farm for paupers, at Tooting in 1849. The
inquests led to the trial for manslaughter, at the Old Bailey, of
the proprietor, a Mr. Drouet. Now, three lengthy essays on this
case, by Dickens, have long been known—more than he ever
wrote on any other such incident; and it now appears that he
wrote a fourth, which takes its place in the whole series, "The
Paradise at Tooting," "The Tooting Farm," "The Recorder's
Charge," and "The Verdict for Drouet." [11] They are an extraor-
dinarily powerful series of essays, marked by Dickens's wit,
scorn, satire, and contempt for the institutions of a society which

[11] All written for the *Examiner* (which was edited by Forster) and dated January
20, January 27, March 3, and April 21, 1849. The new essay is the third, and it
was found—with my help—by Mr. A. W. C. Brice. We expect to edit and reprint
it, as well as other newly identified essays by Dickens. They are mostly about
social causes, education, crime, public health, and the law.

could allow so many children to be so weakened by starvation and neglect that they could so easily be swept away by cholera. They deserve to be read as part of the work of the man who created Squeers from Shaw, and who was to be so concerned in *Little Dorrit* that such tragedies could be "Nobody's Fault." Yet the biographical interest in Dickens's concern lies also in the way in which it was bound into his whole life. He was in the throes of *David Copperfield* at this time: the first number was announced for sale on May 1 and not half finished by April 19. Yet Drouet was acquitted on April 14; Dickens wrote "The Verdict for Drouet" (for publication by the 21st) while worrying about *Copperfield;* and then, on the 18th, he had a large dinner-party at which he was still so eloquent on the trial (or the room was so hot) that two of his most eminent guests collapsed and had to be carried out! They were brought round, and the rest of the dinner-table pulled Dickens's leg and said he was like Drouet, he starved his guests and ill-treated them! [12]

The very next day he complained of his difficulties with the novel, remarking that "the long Copperfieldian perspective is snowy and thick"; and the *next* day there was the christening dinner for his son Henry Fielding, named as "a kind of homage to the style of the work," says Forster, that he "was now so bent on beginning." It is clear that, desperate as Dickens was to get on with the novel, and involved as he was in domestic affairs, he could still make time for expressing his outrage at injustice; and the way in which these events interlock may suggest how his biting satire of "The Paradise at Tooting" at least partly arose from his own childhood experiences, when he felt that he him-

[12] Forster, *Life,* p. 526.

self might have been outcast or lost. The essays make particular play with the link between the children's deaths and social and political injustice. So that the same man who felt driven to write for the weekly press when he was burning to get on with his novel naturally turns from concern for himself to sympathy for others, and then turns back once more to his own work of the imagination which was itself partly composed of pages from his autobiography. This is only one example of how his mind was simultaneously engaged with social causes, himself, and the world of his fiction at this time.

Yet we sometimes hear of how the Dickens of the later novels had a finer awareness of social justice, and that Pip was a sort of apology for "Mealy Potatoes." I am not at all sure that this is simply so. One may believe this, and contrast (say) Magwitch with Micawber; but, even so, it must be allowed that the author of *Great Expectations* had sacrificed a campaign against injustice to a triumph on the stage. The extent of Dickens's personal involvement with his own times, especially in the crucial late forties, has not yet been fully appreciated even by those interested in it; nor, perhaps, the comparative extent to which he gave it up. In the year he began *Copperfield,* for example, several articles on social questions are known. It may be that quite as many more can be shown to be his that are still unknown, generally on crime, ignorance, education, and institutional oppression. If this is so, it may appear that when he came to understand himself better he also lost interest in exploiting this side of his nature; and he did so just because he realized what he was doing. His increased self-knowledge and the way in which the later novels are consequently in some ways more interesting possibly had to be paid for in this way. This may then also suggest that to understand Dickens fully, in his middle period, we sometimes need to supplement the novels. His sympathy and his satire or irony are all part of the man, the way he wrote, and the whole way he looked at life.

It would be possible to trace the extent to which he came to examine himself as well as society in his minor pieces, though we also can fairly dispense with it. Yet it was a continuous element in his writing. Nothing could be less true of these later essays, and of the novels themselves, than to believe (as Kathleen Tillotson does of Dickens of the early period) that he drew on his memories "surreptitiously" or without being fully "aware" of it.[13] Looking back has a particular fascination for essayists, but for Dickens this came to be more personal than generalized. He mentions in his letters how, when his sister was dying, the memory of their childhood brought back the smell of the wet leaves they had once walked through; his thoughts in the semifictional Christmas story of "The Holly Tree" (1855) are all of his own past, including the freely written account of how he used constantly to dream of Mary Hogarth until he told his wife, when the dreams vanished; there are accounts of how he could speak and think in Italian when in the intermediate state between sleeping and waking, though he had long grown rusty in its use; there is the strange tale of a childhood memory of a one-legged man in a coal cellar, which he was able to recall in his sister though they both were quite unable to account for it. These experiences were all part of his life, as much as his "old way home by the Borough" that he wrote made him "cry" after

[13] *Novels of the Eighteen-Forties* (Oxford, 1954), p. 109.

his "eldest child could speak," and his saying that he often wandered "desolately back to that time" in his dreams.[14] The sound of someone playing *Masaniello* on the piano stopped him short in a letter to Forster (in 1857) and reminded him of his childhood and of his nurse's singing him the Evening Hymn— so he says, writing "from Gadshill, September 24, 1857; 'Being here again, or as much here as anywhere in particular.'" A whole series of essays in the early numbers of *Household Words* shows Dickens turning back to the past, perhaps through the association of reliving it for *David Copperfield:* "A Child's Dream of a Star" has its memories of the same sister, "Our Watering Place" partly glances back, and so do "Our School," "The Flight," "A Christmas Tree," and "The Holly Tree." One of the last of these *Reprinted Pieces* to be printed ("The Long Voyage," December 31, 1853) is placed first in the collection, and ends: "I stand upon a seashore, where the waves are years. They break and fall, and I may little heed them; but, with every wave the sea is rising, and I know that it will float me on this traveller's voyage at last."

Familiar, too, is the essay in the *Uncommercial Traveller,* "Travelling Abroad," in which Dickens meets himself as a small boy outside Gad's Hill Place on his way to Dover and is told by the boy that his father had said that if he worked hard he might come to live in a house like that. The past, as Kathleen Tillotson again says, may seem to be "encountered" by Dickens here rather than "remembered." [15] Yet Dickens himself encountered it in the essay only because his memories made him seek out the past

14 Forster, *Life,* p. 26.

15 *Novels of the Eighteen-Forties,* p. 109.

at a time when this house happened to be for sale; and this was only because he had evidently chosen to spend his forty-third birthday, in February, walking along "between walls of snow . . . from three to six feet high," down the same road that he had once known as a boy and back down which he had recently sent David Copperfield.[16]

It was clearly, by this time, a most self-conscious if obsessive return to the past. We can fully believe the autobiographical account that he often revisited scenes of his London childhood by night, just as in the *Uncommercial Traveller* and in *Household Words* we find him going back to Chatham, recalling memories of birthdays and New Year's Day, of children's stories, of "my first funeral," and (in *Household Words*) in "Gone Astray" telling the story of how as a boy he was once lost in London. By the time of *Little Dorrit* it would seem that Dickens even took Forster with him to look over the London scenes of his childhood, and evidently to Bayham Street where the family first lived, for Dickens told him then that to look over "the dust-heaps and dock-leaves and fields" as a child, at St. Paul's, had been "a treat that served him for hours of vague reflection afterwards." [17]

It cannot be surprising, therefore, when we turn to *Little Dorrit,* to find it very much a novel of the past, of memory, and

---

[16] There are at least two versions of how Dickens came to buy Gad's Hill. One, usually followed by biographers, is based on a letter to his friend de Cerjat (January 17, 1857) and places it in the summer of 1855 when, as Dickens explained, he "happened to be walking past," when it was up for sale. That this is wrong is shown by Dickens's letters to Miss Coutts (February 9, 1855) and to W. H. Wills (same date). See *Letters,* ed. W. Dexter (London, 1938).

[17] Forster, *Life,* p. 11.

deeply concerned with how to treat a determined dwelling on past wrongs and seeking for past happiness. "Where We Stopped Growing" would be an entirely apt description of Dickens's state of mind at this time, as long as it is remembered that he was almost entirely conscious of it.

The novel is as saturated with a sense of past Time as *Copperfield*. Sometimes, in fact, the allusions are too obvious and rhetorical: as when Dickens winds up the tension which shall carry the story forward in a fresh number (No. V, ch. 15) with the warning:

> Time shall show us. The post of honour and the post of shame . . . a peer's statue in Westminster Abbey and a seaman's hammock in the bosom of the deep, the mitre and the workhouse . . . the throne and the guillotine . . . the travellers to all are on the great high road . . . and only Time shall show us whither.

Other main thematic signposts are the use of the river, to mean something even more than the passage of time, more even than its momentary continuity as Arthur remains on the bank poised between future and the past which so heavily weighs on him; and the ominous initials D.N.F. (*Do Not Forget*) in the watch sent by her husband to Mrs. Clennam which have a multiple significance. Nothing, again, is more suggestive of past Time than the house of Clennam which will collapse before its occupants at last, and leave them all in dust. It seems haunted by rustling figures of the past, which make the dust drop softly and seem to hold its doors close. Repeatedly, too, as we pass through the various cities in the story we are led to see their inhabitants as survivors from the past only "encamped" within them. The "poor people" of Bleeding Heart Yard have "set up their rest among its faded glories, as Arabs of the desert pitch their tents among the fallen stones of the Pyramids." The "venerable inhabitants" of Hampton Court seem "to be encamped there like . . . civilised gipsies"; while Miss Wade, near Park Lane, lives as "in an Eastern caravanserai." When the Dorrits pass to Rome and Venice, they find cities where "everything seemed to be trying to stand still for ever on the ruins of something else"; and where, to Little Dorrit, the ruins of the past are like the ruins of the Marshalsea. Yet, unlike Little Dorrit herself, who finds that the ruins of Rome correspond to "the unreality of her own inner life," its other pilgrim visitors can make no contact between their present and Rome's past. "Blindfolded moderns carefully" feel "their way" through "the rugged remains," firmly declining to bring their judgment to bear on the past—particularly Mrs. General, who occupies herself in "scratching up the driest little bones of antiquity, and bolting them whole without any human visitings—like a Ghoule in gloves."

I would like to elaborate further—but for Time itself—on the skill with which *Little Dorrit* plays with Time: how it is associated with a sense of place not only in the houses of Clennam and Casby but in London itself; the way in which it is interwoven with the language; and the use of watches and clocks for ceaselessly measuring Time which, otherwise, sometimes seems almost to have stopped. But it is the attitude to the past of some of the major characters which is most revealing. It is especially clear in Flora and Mrs. Clennam—again, something like the Woman in White and the Woman in Black; yet, again, this is so obvious as not to need elaboration, except to remind us how persistently it is woven into the pattern of the novel. Flora has "left about half of herself at eighteen years of age behind, and grafted the rest on to the relict of the late Mr. F; thus making a moral mermaid of herself." Her constant routine with Arthur is to put "herself and him in their old places," and to go through "all the old performances—now when the stage was dusty, when the scenery was faded . . . when the lights were out." Mrs. Clennam stays unmoved: for fifteen years nothing about her has altered. "She is as she always is now," says Flintwinch, and everything is as it has been "night and day for fifteen years." As soon as she and her son speak, "the old influence of her presence and her stern strong voice, so gathered about [him] that he felt conscious of a renewal of the timid chill and reserve of his childhood." As she reads at evening prayers, "years seemed to fall away from [him] like the imaginings of a dream, and all the old dark horrors of his usual preparation for the sleep of an innocent child to overshadow him."

Clearly, Miss Wade's actions are also determined by her past, so much so that, to make this clear, we have her presenting her own written autobiography, in improbable circumstances, to someone she distrusts. This stopping "the clock of busy existence" (as we have been told) is a "mental unhealthiness"—a disease which has stopped their "growing" quite as much as Maggie's, who says, "Oh, it's all very fine for you, little mother . . . but I'm a poor thing only ten years old." Clearly, too, it is part of the pattern that Amy is the counterpart of Maggie: the childlike figure who is a woman, and the woman, physically developed but mentally a child.

It is in the Dorrits, too, that this attitude to the past is so revealing. Amy and Uncle Frederick accept the past: she is even obsessed by it, and he bursts out upon the others with the cry "Have you no memory, have you no heart?" They, of course, once they have come to riches, are determined to forget the past. Fanny's part in the novel is developed about her first having known Mrs. Merdle and Mr. Sparkler as a dancer, and her refusal to admit it once she is an heiress. But it is in William Dorrit that we have the most powerful presentation of a man who, as a prisoner, is first sentimentally tearful that his children will never know him as he really was "unless my face, when I am dead, subsides into the long departed look"; then, after his inheritance, outrageously denies the past, as when he turns on young John Chivery as he arrives bearing him cigars and memories; and who, finally, has his wish exactly fulfilled when in dying he forsakes the present.

It is here that we can turn, for a moment, from interpretation to biography, in order to comment on the usually accepted identification of William Dorrit with John Dickens, which has affected some readings of the novel. For their only association is that both were imprisoned as debtors in the Marshalsea; unless it is insisted that both are seen as parents, and that both are confirmed borrowers—though they could hardly have been debtors if they had not been. Yet it is hardly enough to say that William Dorrit is just an unsympathetic impression of the same man seen more happily as Micawber. John Dickens *was* like Micawber; he was meant to be; both Dickens and Forster remark on it; their speech is meant to be alike; and both of them are seen as open and cheerful borrowers, who did not just hint about "testimonials." Dickens, moreover, respected his father; and, while it is the essence of Dorrit that he comes into riches, goes traveling abroad, and denies the past, John Dickens after all never did do so. The one number of the Dickens family who did was Charles Dickens himself. So, while not simply putting forward an alternative "Dickens original," I must agree with Edgar Johnson's comment in his biography of Dickens that there was less of his father than of Charles Dickens himself in William Dorrit; and that it came from the realization that at this time (as we have seen) he was both living on the past and refusing to acknowledge it; and that, for example, he could no more have admitted that he once gave a low bow in return to a half-crown tip than William Dorrit could face young Chivery.

Yet, wrong as it would be to read *Little Dorrit* as if it were entirely peopled with new Dickens "originals," it is still strongly personal, and the autobiography is diffused through the whole book. At times, too, there is an intentional confusion between superficial present and remembered past, common to human experience. For Arthur Clennam (as we have seen) can be driven back into the past by the mere force of association: at one point he even feels that he has married the dead Meagles twin-sister, whom he has never met. Little Dorrit, in Italy, feels as if she is in a dream and "only the old mean Marshalsea a reality"—and as if, at any moment, her carriage might "bring up with a jolt" at its gate. One might accumulate instances. Yet it is chiefly with Amy Dorrit that there is the most persuasive sense of identification.

For there is surely a strong association between the fictional character who can write of the Marshalsea, "I have often dreamed of myself back there seeing faces in the yard little known," and the man who said that his "old way home" as a child, from the same prison, "made me cry after my eldest child could speak"; between the one who writes, "I often look up at the stars . . . and believe that I am in the street" outside, and the other who wrote, "I often forget in my dreams that I am a man . . . and wander desolately back to that time of life." Some of the interest we feel in reading the novel, as well as the embarrassment that I believe we share—as, for example, at Arthur's total collapse ("a ruined man whose course is run, who asks to be remembered only as I am")—is possibly wrung from us because of Dickens's personal involvement with its situations.

For as well as being about characters who refuse to accept the past, the novel—as far as it concerns both Arthur Clennam and Little Dorrit—is also largely about the return to the scene of an unhappy and even wronged childhood to find freedom and fulfillment. Of the two characters, toward the end of the novel, it probably becomes easier for the reader to identify with Arthur, since the story is more often told from his point of view. Yet, in addition, Arthur is required by the development of the story to be brought to accept that he is neither so old, nor so bound by the past, that family, institutions, or society should restrict his life. It is reasonable to see this as related to Dickens's own changing sense of purpose, for he would have gladly been free of all these encumbrances. Yet the attempt to show Arthur Clennam's rebirth is done both in terms of his personal development and with religious overtones; and, although this is skillfully done, the novel is surely most successful when simply looking to the past. It is true that we may regard *Little Dorrit* as to some degree religious in feeling, and define it as "a novel about the will and society"; but, comparatively, this leaves out too much. Indeed, in so far as we are meant to see Amy Dorrit as like the Holy Spirit, or our attention is directed to the crown of thorns which appears in the sky as she and Mrs. Clennam leave the Marshalsea, these have little to do even with Arthur's redemption. The Christian symbols are used here (as perhaps sometimes in other novels) almost parasitically. It is true that a converted Christian should be able to forgive and to begin a new life, but doubtful whether Arthur is enough of an Everyman, or vital enough in his redemption, for the novel to be effectively read as if both Christian and religious.

Of course, other novels can be thought of in a somewhat similar way, and *Great Expectations* easily comes to mind. *A Tale of Two Cities* makes even more dramatic use of a man who has suffered "a great wrong" and who is driven back into the past however much he struggles against it. Yet there was a limit to the extent that this experience could be worked without repetition; and, even more, perhaps, the very intensity with which Dickens dealt with it in *David Copperfield* and *Little Dorrit* changed his own response. We may reasonably be reminded of how, having dreamed for years of his own dead sister-in-law, Mary Hogarth, he had only to tell his wife about it for the dreams to stop. So, although *Our Mutual Friend* uses some of the same themes, it does so less intensely. Some of its characters do still seek to cancel the past (as John Harmon or Charley Hexam), or they ask riddles about Time (as Eugene or Jenny Wren); and it is Riah (himself "like the ghost of a Departed Time") who is sharply told by Jenny that his conventional consolation about lost happiness means that "You had better change Is into Was and Was into Is, and keep them so."

The later works are not all of a piece—and it is likely that Dickens had come to recognize that only in fiction could Jenny's advice be taken literally, and that (though for a time he had sought to accomplish it) even in fiction dreams and reality are hard to reconcile.

Alan Trachtenberg

THE JOURNEY BACK: MYTH AND HISTORY

IN *Tender Is the Night*

LIKE MANY AMERICAN WRITERS, Scott Fitzgerald had considerable difficulty in arriving at a reliable and comfortable form for his novels. Uncertainty about form is usually a sign of crisis in the development of an artist; in the case of novelists the crisis is often in a shifting conception of society, a changing vision of the relations between individual minds and the collective mind. Fitzgerald's entire fiction is an extended meditation on America, its history and its notorious dreams, a meditation all the more remarkable for its multiple moods of elegy, prayer, social analysis, and introspection. But difficulties with form in specific works suggest an underlying hesitation or uncertainty in Fitzgerald about his heroes and their place within American society—an uncertainty rooted in part in profound ambivalence regarding his own popular success and his promise. In the several instances in which his fictions do achieve a balance between reflective subjectivity and objective detachment, as in *The Great Gatsby* and *Tender Is the Night,* the resulting forms are fully convincing embodiments of a complex and difficult vision.

Fitzgerald's meditation often brings into focus a tension between history and dreams, between the corrosive action of time and the illusory nature of myth. If his theme is frequently disappointment in the failure of the American Dream to realize itself within history, then a conflict between history and myth as opposing ways of viewing the world lies at the heart of his vision.

The relation between history and myth is often confused by the suggestion that one is "true," the other "false." In fact, however, both terms refer to states of mind, to conditions or modes of consciousness, to points of view toward experience. The meaningful difference between them lies elsewhere than in their relation to literal "facts" in the world. The term myth has been subject to a bewildering assault of definitions; perhaps the most useful is that myth refers to experiences timeless in nature—experiences of thought, feeling, and imagination outside a linear chronicle of events. Any recurrent pattern can thus be described as mythic. In an influential essay Allen Tate argues that "literature as knowledge" is knowledge of a "mythical order," an order in which, as Mr. Tate quotes I. A. Richards, "the opposite and discordant qualities in things . . . acquire a form." [1] Myth is accordingly a cognitive mode, a way of knowing.

We need to recognize that history can have the same status, as a way of thinking about the world: not how the world actually organizes itself, but how it gets organized in our minds. Like myth, history is a dimension of consciousness. The distinguishing trait of historical as opposed to mythic awareness is that it accepts

[1] *The Man of Letters in the Modern World* (New York, 1955), p. 63.

the reality of time, irreducibly. Also, a historical awareness accepts the idea that things exist "out there," independent of our perceptions, that they change and organize themselves in certain concrete ways. A sense of history need not imply a specific system of explanation, but it must grant an "out there" with a significant, even if problematic, relevance to "in here." Myth tends to diminish the value of separate moments of experience by bringing them into a pre-existing pattern of coherence, while history tends to enhance the value of time as change, even if, in some troubled periods, it deplores both time and change. Myth and history may stand against each other as ways of knowing the world, but both are relevant to the experience of literature.

For Fitzgerald, history and myth provide perspectives upon each other, mutual contexts in which the opposition is rarely simple. He requires his reader to recognize each perspective, to identify the tension and experience it dramatically. The problem is perhaps clearer to demonstrate in *The Great Gatsby*. For example, after one of his parties, themselves extravagant versions of the exchange between the myth of plenitude and the fact of stolen wealth in America, Jay Gatsby strolls with Nick Carraway "up and down a desolate path of fruit rinds and discarded favors and crushed flowers." The images establish an undercurrent of wastage which questions plenitude, of loss and futility in the action of time upon the frangible substance of dream. In this ambiguous setting Gatsby makes Nick an intimate to his bewildered feeling that Daisy no longer understands him. He wants her not only to leave Tom but to renounce her husband altogether, to deny she ever loved him. Then she and Gatsby can return to Louisville to resume their old affair as if the interval of five years had not occurred. Nick, the historical voice of the book, offers an obvious comment: " 'You can't repeat the past.' " Gatsby's reply reveals how deeply the words torment him:

> "Can't repeat the past?" he cried incredulously. "Why of course you can!"
>
> He looked around him wildly, as if the past were lurking here in the shadow of his house, just out of reach of his hand.[2]

The confused energy of his response carries a dark intimation of debacle, of a violent incursion of history upon dream.

The reader's work here and throughout the book is to balance his simultaneous recognition of Gatsby's banality and his transcendence. The issue focuses on the word "repeat," on its trite yet audacious denial of the linear movement of events. Gatsby's fantasy of renewal is based on a pristine hope in a future which will restore a past intact and untarnished. In the simplicity of this hope—not merely or even primarily for Daisy, but for a victory over time itself—we detect desperation. Fitzgerald sees time as a depriver; the passage of time can mean only loss for Gatsby. But Gatsby represents extreme ranges of behavior: he has more to lose in time because he has more to gain in his challenge of time, if he can indeed "repeat the past." Without an illusion like his, historical experience is barren. Yet to possess such a fervent illusion is to be susceptible to disaster.

---

[2] *The Great Gatsby* (New York, 1925). All quotations are from the Scribner Library edition (1953) and are used by permission of Charles Scribner's Sons.

Survival requires energies and tensities quite different from his, the possessions of a Buchanan or a Wolfsheim, and in another sense, of a Carraway. As the illusion of regaining Daisy becomes insupportable, Gatsby's "old warm world" of his dream crumbles into "a new world, material without being real." What had begun as an "incarnation" when he first kissed Daisy, completes itself five years later as a "holocaust."

Gatsby tries to work with the materials of time for radically atemporal purposes. As a true believer in his dream, he has already deprived himself of a historical sense, the kind of sense which in the end saves Nick by allowing him to place the myth in the context of history. Nick's vision of the Dutch sailors contemplating the virgin wilderness permits him to recognize the historical, that is, the *American,* meanings of Gatsby's experience. That final vision is subtly foreshadowed earlier when Nick perceives that Gatsby's dream was to "recover some idea of himself, perhaps, that had gone into loving Daisy." If history is loss, then historical action might be recovery. The backward thrust, however, wants really to stop history, to turn it about. Its motive is mythical rather than historical. Moreover, Gatsby's elaborate strategies of recovery clarify a buried behavior pattern in his entire culture. What he performs as a pure and purifying ritual has its degraded and corrupt counterparts in the characteristic behavior of his milieu (Nick is an exception: he is "reminded of something" he "had heard long ago" by Gatsby's account of kissing Daisy). The frenzy in the life surrounding Gatsby enacts the quest for recovery as parody. Like its elegant roughneck hero, the book's world has deprived itself of conscious historical experience—it prefers the "sensation" of "Vladimir Tostoff's

Jazz History of the World," or furniture like Myrtle's, tapestried with "scenes of ladies swinging in the garden of Versailles"—in order to pursue one or another debased version of the dream of incarnation (see Myrtle's list in Chapter Two of "all the things I've got to get"). No genuine historical future seems available, unless it be Nick's deliberate retreat from the recklessness of such a world. The elegiac tone of the book's ending confirms Nick's final insight, that history, in America at least, is a record of struggles to recover the past in the future, to recapture the fleeting moments of wonder when victory over time seemed possible. But the ongoing currents of time, he realizes, will always defeat such an "orgiastic future."

To a great extent the reader relies on Nick for a balanced perspective—one which locates Gatsby at the intersection of two vectors, the pull of dream and the push of time. In *Tender Is the Night* the perspective does not come as easily; it lies in wait for the reader and requires a different kind of activity from him. The difference is almost entirely a matter of a new emphasis given to the historical perspective. Nick's narrative is retrospective and suggestively static; the actions come to us with the clarity and sharpness of formal postures. The later novel, on the other hand, can be described as a novel of process; its actions appear more fluid and casual. But at the same time its movements are more elaborately and calculatedly subtle and complex. What reaches the reader through the consciousness of Nick in the earlier novel, the reader of *Tender Is the Night* must attain for himself. The experience is more difficult, but the rewards justify the kind of attention the book demands, and too rarely receives.

The larger demands, and the different kind of historical awareness in *Tender,* can be introduced by a brief passage from Book Two. Dick Diver has just buried his father in an old churchyard in Virginia. As he prepares to leave he becomes aware of the other buried souls, "made of new earth in the forest-heavy darkness of the seventeenth century," and takes his farewell: " 'Good-by, my father—good-by, all my fathers.' " This scene marks the final break with his personal American past; it sets the stage for his ill-fated fling in Rome in the next episode. In the passage immediately following "good-by," Dick begins to make his way from his old New World to a new Old one:

> On the long-roofed steamship piers one is in a country that is no longer here and not yet there. The hazy yellow vault is full of echoing shouts. There are the rumble of trucks and the clump of trucks, the strident chatter of cranes, the first salt smell of the sea. One hurries through, even though there's time; the past, the continent, is behind; the future is the glowing mouth in the side of the ship; the dim, turbulent alley is too confusedly the present.[3]

The imagery of ambiguous time-dimensions on the pier connects the specific narrative moment, Dick's farewell journey, with basic confusions in his sense of time itself. The haze and the echoes in the turbulent vault convey a feeling of literal confusion, of a mixture of tenses (echoes implying the past haunting the present). The sentence, "One hurries through, even though there's time," suggests dislocation, a serious disjunction

---

[3] *Tender Is the Night* (New York, 1934). All quotations are from the Scribner Library edition and are used by permission of Charles Scribner's Sons.

between time and emotion. The country of the steamship pier
defines Dick's condition by objectifying an inner confusion of
identities. By means of these images (which have, of course, a
yet wider context within the entire narrative), the reader is able
to, in fact must, see the concrete fact of Dick's farewell journey
in light of the accompanying fact of a confused sense of time.
Thus "history" develops two mutually reinforcing meanings:
Dick's relation to a specific past, now "behind" him; and his
(and our) sense of the disordered structure of the present. The
second meaning becomes, in short, the form through which we
become aware of the first: the farewell journey becomes equiva-
lent to a dislocated sense of historical time.

The relations among the reader, the imagery, and the action
have a different tension here than in *Gatsby*. The difference represents an important shift—as Fitzgerald himself put it, an "advance"—in his understanding of his theme of history and myth
in America. In this book, a special kind of historical awareness,
created by the reader in the act of reading, becomes the major
perspective of the narrative. In order to make this difficult point
as clear as possible, we need first to consider more carefully the
relevance of "history" to fiction.

"All works of the mind," writes Jean-Paul Sartre, "contain
within themselves the image of the reader for whom they are intended." Sartre continues, in "For Whom Does One Write?",[4]
to establish an important connection between the imagined reader
and the historical dimension of literature. Before considering the
implications of that connection, I want to cite a number of in-

[4] *What Is Literature?* (New York, 1965), Chapter 3.

stances which demonstrate Fitzgerald's own acute awareness of the intended reader of *Tender Is the Night*. Fitzgerald belongs with Henry James among the most conscious and scrupulous craftsmen in American literature, and his comments upon craft, almost invariably practical and concrete, indicate his ability to think about his work from the point of view of a reader. "The novel should do this," he began his "General Plan" for *Tender* in 1932, an expression which emphasizes his sense of the book as an action upon a reader.

In 1925, fresh from the success of *The Great Gatsby*, Fitzgerald promised impetuously that his next book would be "something really NEW in form, idea, structure—the model for the age that Joyce and Stein are searching for, that Conrad didn't find." [5] It would be, he wrote at the same time, "the most amazing form ever invented." Discussing the finished product in 1934, Fitzgerald had subdued his exuberance somewhat—sobered no doubt by the enormous difficulties of composition—but he insisted in a letter to John Peale Bishop that the book was a definite "advance" over *Gatsby*. His explanation was largely technical; the book's importance, he felt, lay chiefly in its form. "The intention in the two books," he wrote to Bishop, "was entirely different." The compressed, highly compacted method of the first work had come to seem too limited. "The dramatic novel," he continued, "has canons quite different from the philosophical, now called psychological, novel. One is a kind of *tour de force* and the other a confession of faith. It would be like comparing a sonnet sequence with an epic." The mention of

---

[5] *The Letters of F. Scott Fitzgerald*, ed. Andrew Turnbull (New York, 1963), p. 182. Quotations are used by permission of Charles Scribner's Sons.

epic indicates a larger scale and scope in the new book: not only
a larger segment of time (one summer in *Gatsby,* several years
in *Tender*), but a more historical perspective as well. Unlike
the epic form, however, this work would deal with very contemporary material, a fact which required that he deliberately
refrain from "pointing up" dramatic scenes. He was able to get
away with that in *Gatsby,* he points out, because the material
was essentially exotic. But here, "the material itself was so har-
rowing and highly charged that I did not want to subject the
reader to a series of nervous shocks in a novel that was inevitably close to whoever read it in my generation." [6] The reference to nervous shocks is itself striking in light of the fact that
the novel is in part a record of the strained state of nerves in
Fitzgerald's marriage, a record whose honesty might indeed
shock a reader close to the original events. But the brunt of the
sentence is that the novel is decidedly not a case study, that the
author wished to avoid exploiting obvious sensational possibilities, and that a certain distance between the reader and the
events was a deliberate and necessary feature of the novel's
form.

In the same letter Fitzgerald justifies his use of what he calls
the "dying fall" as preferable to the "dramatic ending," and his
concern for the peculiar nature of the novel's material vis-à-vis
the reader is equally evident. Writing to Hemingway a few
weeks later, he confesses to have "stolen" this device from him
and cites Conrad's Preface to *The Nigger of the Narcissus* as
the original source of the theory that "the purpose of a work of
fiction is to appeal to the lingering after-effects in the reader's

[6] *Ibid.,* p. 363.

mind as differing from, say, the purpose of oratory or philosophy which respectively leave people in a fighting or thoughtful mood." In the last pages of *Tender,* Fitzgerald explains, he wants to tell the reader that "after all, this is just a casual event," and "to let *him* come to bat for *me* rather than going out to shake his nerves, whoop him up, then leaving him rather in a condition of a frustrated woman in bed." [7]

Aside from the specific technical issues these comments raise, it is clear that Fitzgerald felt that the differences in scope and in materials between *Gatsby* and *Tender* amounted to a different relationship to an imagined reader, that is, a different kind of form. An imagined reader gives to the material a particularity, the possibility of a concrete form. With this in mind, we can return to Sartre, who writes that books serve as "go-betweens," establishing "a historical contact among men who are steeped in the same history and who likewise contribute to its making. Writing and reading are two facets of the same historical fact." By "historical fact" Sartre means the very act of reading, an act to which both writer and reader contribute. The book converts the abstract relation between writer and reader—a relation of separateness—into a concrete one; the book gives the relationship a particularity, an exact form. Moreover, the aesthetic experience which is the product of reading, Sartre argues, is an experience of freedom, of liberation from the oppression and alienation of the "normal" world of history in which both writer and reader are separately "steeped." The freedom won in writing-reading is likewise concrete and particular. It is not, Sartre insists in his existentialist vocabulary, "a pure abstract

[7] *Ibid.,* pp. 309–10.

consciousness of being free," but, "strictly speaking, it *is* not; it wins itself in a historical situation"—which is the concrete situation, or experience, of the book.

But what do we mean by describing a fiction as a "historical situation" in itself? It is obvious that the act of reading can be considered "historical" because it occurs in a specific time and place, because it influences the sense of reality of the reader, and in turn is influenced by the historical limitations of the reader (accounting, for example, for the seriously altered ways Shakespeare is read and performed from age to age). These are, however, contextual versions of "history"; they place the act of reading within a clearly defined setting. But what occurs within that setting has a structure and a coherence of its own, a structure which requires the reader to suspend, to struggle against, his ordinary sense of time. A fictive time structure by itself, of course, is not yet a "history." Carl Becker defined history as "the memory of things said and done." The definition can be usefully applied to fictions. Plots, for example, rely upon a reader's memory as the continuous element in the unfolding of events page by page. Plots require a historical memory, that is, a memory provoked and directed and supplied by the fiction itself. True, fictions often call upon a larger social memory "of things said and done" which the reader can be counted on to bring to the book, but the concrete history within which, in Sartre's terms, the reader's "consciousness of being free" wins itself is created by and contained within the fiction itself. The meaningful "historical situation" of a fiction, then, is that which it creates for itself in collaboration with a reader.

If a fiction is a history, however, it is so in a very specialized and, in a significant sense, unstable way. The ordinary sense of history can be described as consciousness of a sequence of non-repeatable events, related to each other as chronology and, in some minds, as causality. Mere chronology is quite obviously an inadequate structure for a plot, which requires some comprehensible system of causality. A plot will tend to structure events on the basis of congruences, recognitions, reversals, will tend to pattern our perceptions and thus contribute an element of geometry to our awareness of events (including mental events). Temporal awareness begins to bend toward spatial awareness, and history may be in danger of becoming geometry. In "Spatial Form in Modern Literature," Joseph Frank argued that the inherent geometric tendency in plots contributed to a virtual revolution in modern literature, a revolution directed against nineteenth-century historicism and its faith in linear causality. In modern fiction and poetry, he pointed out, myth, in the form of archetypes or prototypes, tends to replace history as the source of significance. The works of Joyce and Eliot, for example, require the reader to perceive resemblances between present and archetypal events not as temporal facts, occurring in linear sequence, but as spatial facts: not as history repeating itself but as history being always fundamentally the same. This procedure in reading modern literature assumes that coherence in our perceptions about ourselves and our world cannot derive from the events themselves but from some atemporal pattern in which the events participate. "The objective historical imagination," writes Frank, has given way to a mythological imagination "for which historical time does not exist." [8]

The "historical situation" of a fiction can, therefore, contain

[8] "Spatial Form in Modern Literature," in *Criticism, The Foundations of Modern Literary Judgment,* eds. Mark Schorer, Josephine Miles, Gordon McKenzie (New York, 1948), pp. 379–92.

a radically ahistorical experience. This point becomes significant in evaluating the differences once more between *Tender Is the Night* and *The Great Gatsby*. In many ways *Gatsby* is a predominantly spatial form, and *Tender* predominantly temporal. Much of the activity of reading *Gatsby* is taken up with recognitions of symbolic values in the book's geography, in the historical prototypes and mythic archetypes lurking behind Jay Gatsby. Gatsby himself is a character for whom "historical time does not exist." His aspiration toward the past is fully mythic, an aspiration toward a timeless condition, toward a redemption of the unalterable sequence of time, toward a virtually ritualistic "return" to an original incarnation. Of course the novel does not grant him his aspirations, and the terms of his failure are the terms of the book's historical perspective. But that perspective is embodied almost entirely in Nick's point of view, rather than in a process of developing awareness in the reader. The novel concludes at a point which compels us to feel the contours of a historical process behind Gatsby, but the process itself remains off-stage, in a kind of outer darkness. In *Tender Is the Night* Fitzgerald attempted to dramatize the process itself, to bring the on-stage action into a dynamic and intelligible relation to the outer darkness. It remains to examine the technical terms of his attempt and to evaluate its success.

In all cases we submit ourselves to a fiction's pedagogy; we need to learn to become the work's imagined reader. *Tender Is the Night* consists of a great number of episodes connected in seemingly casual and incidental ways. Fitzgerald once commented on his own work: "Whether it's something that happened twenty years ago or only yesterday, I must start out with an emotion—one that's close to me and that I can understand." An emotion is a present experience, a "now," even if it is a reflex or "lingering after-effect" of a past experience. *Tender Is the Night* consists of many "nows"—presents which imply a past. The reader modulates from one to another, experiencing each emotion as an event, and constructing a memory of each separate "now" in developing relations with the others.

The reader's memory is abetted by the narrative's precise chronological structure. The story covers a period from 1917 to 1930, from America's entrance into World War I to the beginning of the Depression. Details from the larger, extra-fictional social memory play at first a relatively inconspicuous role, but in the end they share significantly in the book's historical perspective, linking the career of Dick Diver with the career of American life itself. Most of the action occurs in a four-year period, from 1925 to 1929. The original 1934 version, which I prefer for reasons which will become obvious, is divided into three brooks. Book One opens in 1925; the predominant though not exclusive point of view of the book is Rosemary's, and we see Dick Diver through her infatuated eyes at his apparent best, his charm most engaging, his control most intact. Chinks in his armor begin to appear, however: increasing loss of self-control with Rosemary, and a mysterious difficulty with his wife. The opening episodes also sketch a setting of pleasurable charm mixed with random violence: the duel, the shooting at the railroad station, the murder of the Negro. The climax of the book occurs in the bathroom of the Divers' suite in Paris where Rosemary finally witnesses Nicole's derangement.

Book Two opens in 1917, eight years earlier, with Dick's arrival in Switzerland. The book takes him through his early affair and then his marriage with Nicole, introduces her sister, Baby Warren, and brings the major cast forward, in Chapter 11, to rejoin the present in 1925, immediately following the Paris episode which concluded Book One. Book Two is devoted mainly to Dick's point of view, his sense of himself, and documents the successive stages of his marriage and his decline until the climactic collapse in Rome, where his deterioration and his humiliating attachment to the Warren fortune become most blatantly evident to him and to the reader. The book parallels Book One in several ways. The pastoral isolation of Dick's little clearing on the Riviera beach in the first book is recalled in the isolation of Switzerland from the surrounding violence of the war in the opening paragraphs of Book Two (the allusion to "more intriguing strangers" in the second paragraph of Book Two may be a deliberate echo of "Hôtel des Étrangers" in the first paragraph of Book One); Dick's attachment to Rosemary in Book One brings to mind the early stages of his affair with Nicole in Book Two; and his collapse in Rome virtually parallels Nicole's seizure in Paris after the murder of Peterson. The resemblances, however, serve mainly to reveal important differences between the time periods, differences which point to the unfolding truth of Dick's condition. The resemblances are not geometric repetitions; they serve to indicate a fully temporal process of deterioration in Dick and a corresponding process of illumination in the reader. For example, although the reader is shrewder than Rosemary in Book One and can guess at what expense Dick keeps his charm and his manners apparently intact, the story of his marriage and of the role of Baby Warren traced in the first ten chapters of Book Two begins to clarify those expenses and to prepare the reader to accept knowingly Dick's admission to Mrs. Spears in Chapter 11 (where, remember, we return to the present), " 'My politeness is a trick of the heart.' " The careful structuring of events in the two books gives such revelations a key role in the developing sense of ambiguity in Dick's character and his condition. The structure prepares the reader to receive such statements and to place their emotional tone in a concrete relation to events that have already taken place.

Book Three, deceptively simple in appearance, is the most difficult section of the novel. To deal with its complexities we need to consider more closely the ambiguities surrounding Dick, to see how they develop and how they relate to the narrative structure. So far the novel's movement has been a progressive unfolding (including a retrogressive filling-in of earlier events) of the truth about Dick, his manners, and his marriage. What Rosemary sees in Book One is steadily exposed as appearance or illusion, a partial view of reality. But appearances are not mere disguises. The illusion is very much a part of the total reality of Dick. Rosemary's point of view is an accurate one with which to begin the novel because what she sees is really there, if seriously incomplete. The full picture proceeds to disclose itself, but not mechanically, the way shadowed areas light up to expose in full clarity what was there all the time. Although the revelation is indeed largely retrospective, it develops progressively; the picture fills out in successive events; relationships and feelings change in the course of time. The truth about Dick is not a secret or a puzzle but a process. The value of Rosemary to the reader is that she demonstrates the dangerous partiality of any point of view which takes an appearance for the entire truth. The whole story is the entire history.

For example, if the opening chapters of Book Two, covering the period from 1917 to 1925, require us to understand the events of Book One as consequences of Dick's choices years ago, they also force us to recognize that the consequences have gotten beyond the original range of his choice to marry Nicole. That choice contained potentialities Dick did not realize at the time, potentialities realized only "in time." The realization is never stated explicitly, but becomes part of the reader's growing awareness. By giving us a seriously partial view of the consequences (Book One, especially the affair with Rosemary) before permitting us a larger view of the original choices, Fitzgerald uses a structural distortion of linear time in order to repeat for the reader something like Dick's own process of illusion and disillusion.

A similar process whereby appearances grow ambiguous in the reader's mind is at work in the descriptive imagery. *Gatsby* has an unmistakably symbolic landscape in which values inhere in physical forms (the distinctions between West Egg and East Egg, for example, or the stretch of ashes along the road to New York). In *Tender,* settings contain symbolic suggestions (the "bright tan prayer rug of a beach," for instance), but the suggestions do not comprise a simple moral geography. Instead, landscape is an object of perception; imagery tells how a setting is being perceived, what the perception seizes upon, what it excludes. A dominant feeling in the imagery of a setting may

deliberately obscure certain latent possibilities. The opening
paragraph of Book One exudes a feeling of quiet and wealthy
pleasantness along the Riviera. But contrary muted notes play
along the edge of perception: the façade of the hotel is "flushed,"
the old villas "rotted"—both images unobtrusively injecting
suspicions of disease in a scene of apparent good health, deca-
dence at odds with vitality. Similarly, the delicately cultivated
space on the beach commanded by Dick's rake and tent and
umbrella is defined and conditioned in our awareness by what it
excludes. It excludes and rejects the section further up the beach
"strewn with pebbles and dead sea-weed," where the equally
rejected McKiscos and their crowd sit smoldering in their resentment at Dick's show. " 'We don't know who's in the plot
and who isn't,' " complains Violet McKisco. Dick's space also
excludes the "brutal sunshine" and the "outer, darker sea." The
several exclusions contribute to a scene of virtually theatrical self-
sufficiency and consummate social pleasure: "It seemed that
there was no life anywhere in all this expanse of coast except
under the filtered sunlight of those umbrellas, where something
went on amid the color and the murmur." However, what is
omitted to create such an illusion does not entirely disappear;
the images of the outer world hint at potentialities which five
years later, we learn, will be realized. At the end of the book
(and of Dick's reign), the beach has become a "club," and
"confused shapes and shadows of many umbrellas" now prevail:
"new paraphernalia, the trapezes over the water, the swinging
rings, the portable bathhouses, the floating towers, the search-
lights from last night's fêtes, the modernistic buffet, white with
a hackneyed motif of endless handlebars."

This bizarre setting at the end of Book Three recalls in turn an earlier scene in Paris in Book One. Rosemary had accompanied Dick on a visit to a "house hewn from the frame of Cardinal de Retz's palace"; inside the "long hall of blue steel, silver-gilt, and the myriad facets of many oddly bevelled mirrors," the visitors cannot tell "what this room meant because it was evolving into something else, becoming everything a room was not." The image can be taken as a clue to a process operating within the novel itself. The traditional exterior of the house had become a mere "outer shell," expropriated by the new inhabitants to "enclose the future" ("once inside the door there was nothing of the past, nor of any present that Rosemary knew"), and to cross the threshold is to prepare oneself for the evolutions and expropriations of the novel. It is not surprising, then, that what Dick sees on his beach at the end is a fulfillment, even to the "white sun, chivied of outline by a white sky," of potentialities implicit in the opening paragraphs.

Ambiguity is thus a product of the relation between the surface texture of image and event, the manifest meanings, and the underlying potentialities, the latent meanings. The reader needs to exercise a cautious memory as he moves from page to page, allowing feelings and hints to accumulate. Because each episode, each image, and each feeling will have its fullest reality only within the entire process of the book, each taken by itself is ambiguous—as ambiguous as the illusions which led Dick to Nicole.

Book Three and the meanings of the final actions cannot be understood without a clear sense of the role of ambiguity in the novel. The tension between appearance and latency is one form in which we recognize ambiguity; another is the calculated relationships to each other of three groups of images: of theatrical or cinematic illusion, of war, and of time. A simple summary statement about this configuration is that Dick is an actor whose efforts to serve the illusions of others and to live by his own are progressively eroded by realities represented in images of war and time.

The war imagery is especially effective in connecting Dick's inner life with his outer condition, his dreams with his history. A good example is his curious identification with Ulysses S. Grant. Dick in Zurich is like Grant "lolling in his general store in Galena," about "to be called to an intricate destiny." The image suggests, on one hand, a potentially dangerous tendency in Dick toward self-dramatization, toward a conventional hero-complex. On the other hand, certain genuine parallels begin to develop. Grant's public image shifted in his lifetime from hero to goat. The shift, and Grant's entanglements in the financial scandals of the Gilded Age, suggest a precedent for Dick's own career. If nothing else, the identification implies an inner necessity in Dick to find a "destiny" in Nicole. He sees her at first as "this scarcely saved waif of disaster bringing him the essence of a continent." Her trauma typifies a profound civil war, a clash and confusion of values; her incest with her father brings to the surface a disease already lurking in a civilization where "Daddy's Girl" is a sentimental ideal (" 'People used to say what a wonderful father and daughter we were—they used to wipe their eyes,' " says Devereux Warren). The disease represents an infection in ideals which have lost touch with reality and become outer shells to an inner corruption or an inner emptiness. As a clinical psychiatrist, Dick recognizes that professional logic "tended away from the girl." But a more powerful logic drew him toward her, a logic derived from his American background, from "the illusions of eternal strength and health, and of the essential goodness of people; illusions of a nation, the lies of generations of frontier mothers who had to croon falsely, that there were no wolves outside the cabin door." Himself steeped in such illusions, Dick is drawn to Nicole in part as Grant is drawn to the Civil War; both destinies seem to be opportunities for the exercise of a traditional American ideal, a dedication to the healing of moral wounds.

The intricacy of the destiny is based both on the nature of the wound and on the nature of the dedication. Nicole's wealth and its social character complicate the matter of Dick's motives. To some extent he is "bought"; but he also offers himself to be "used." The allusion to Grant once more helps the reader come to an understanding of the complex issues involved. Grant was called to herohood; in practice, as Dick admits to Abe North, it was Grant's destiny to invent the decidedly unheroic "mass butchery" of Petersburg. Invited by circumstances to play one role, he was compelled by history to play another. At the war memorial of Thiepval Dick laments the passing of a world in which Grant's original kind of heroism was possible; here, he tells Rosemary, "all my beautiful lovely safe world blew itself up with a great gust of high explosive love." The significant implication is that traditional heroic impulses lead in the end to "mass butchery." A corollary in his own life is the fact that his "extraordinary virtuosity with people" becomes an instrument of "carnivals of affection," extravagant parties he looks back on "as a general might gaze upon a massacre he had ordered to satisfy an impersonal blood lust." Led by his need for a heroic role to a highly ambiguous destiny (Nicole's wound and her family wealth), Dick suffers a dislocation; love and heroism and the manners of "essential goodness" have gotten entangled with business. Tommy Barban, Dick's successor, is also his exact foil: fighting in his paying job, not a matter of love or heroism. " 'My business is to kill people.' " Later his business will be stocks and bonds. Tommy is also Grant's foil; the general's destiny was finally to become inept and innocent executor of the most scandalous public corruption of the "new" post-Civil War America. Dick, in turn, was "disgusted" to learn that his own wartime assignment was "executive rather than practical." And as Nicole's husband he serves as an executive officer for the Warrens, in charge of producing health for Nicole.

Dick performs his duties much like an actor or director, thus serving the Warrens and realizing his own idealistic character at the same time. Of the Villa Diana he has made an "intensely calculated perfection," a "stage" where "some memorable thing was sure to happen." The perception here is Rosemary's. Herself a product and servant of the illusion-making industry of Hollywood, Rosemary is well qualified to make these observations, especially because she fails to grasp their full meaning. " 'Oh, we're such actors—you and I,' " she says to Dick, with more wisdom than she realizes. Dick may wince at the sentimentality of her performance in *Daddy's Girl* and recognize that her "triumph" is well coached. But the performance itself, "her fineness of character, her courage and steadfastness intruded upon by the vulgarity of the world," is a sentimentalized

version of his own social "triumph." Rosemary's enactment of
the "illusions of a nation" before the cameras is debased by the
intrinsic insincerity of Hollywood. But have not his own enact-
ments suffered in the service of a social reality he at bottom
cannot accept? For example, his creation, the Villa Diana, disguises the house's true nature: "The villa and its grounds were
made out of a row of peasant dwellings that abutted on the
cliff—five small houses had to be combined to make the house
and four destroyed to make the garden." " 'Nicole's garden,' "
Dick says a moment later.

The tensions between Dick's illusion-making talents and his
objective social role come to a head in Book Three. The book
opens with two observations by the Gregoroviuses, that " 'Nicole's not sick' " but only " 'cherishes her illness as an instrument
of power,' " and that " 'Dick is no longer a serious man.' " The
rest of the book, presented from Nicole's point of view, seems to
extend and qualify these two insights. More and more Nicole
seems to free herself of Dick, who more and more withdraws
into himself. But the structure of the book is not as simple as it
appears. The tantalizing question is precisely what is happening
to Dick as he seems to lose hold of himself and his marriage. In
a letter to his editor, Maxwell Perkins, while the novel was in
proof stage, Fitzgerald insisted on retaining the episode in Book
Three set in Cannes, where Dick saves Mary North and Lady
Caroline Sibly-Biers in their transvestite escapade with the po-
lice. Fitzgerald wanted, he wrote, to show Dick once more as a
dignified and responsible person, in order to point up the fact
that "his intention dominated all this last part." The comment
suggests that Fitzgerald's problem was to strengthen Nicole's

point of view while keeping Dick in the leading role, at the center of the reader's attention and respect.

Like Rosemary's and Dick's in the earlier books, Nicole's point of view in Book Three is not the sole perspective. The reader has been creating what might be called a perspective of the story as a whole, a perspective which contains each separate point of view as it does each separate episode. The way Nicole sees the world has a social history and a social content developed within the process of the narrative. As we have seen in the shifting patterns of imagery, a basic feature of that process is the instability of appearances. Apparently dominant facts and impressions contain opposite possibilities, as the book's present contains a thoroughly unlikely future. Thus the pathos of a sick Nicole, a "waif of disaster," had obscured the potentiality of a healthy Nicole. In Book One, in an intrusive but remarkable passage, we learn to anticipate the restoration of Nicole's social history: she was, we learn, "the product of much ingenuity and toil," an expression, even in her trauma, of an entire social system, for whose sake "trains began their run at Chicago . . . chicle factories fumed . . . men mixed toothpaste in vats . . . girls canned tomatoes . . . half-breed Indians toiled on Brazilian coffee plantations. . . ." Thus "she illustrates very simple principles, containing in herself her own doom, but illustrated them so accurately that there was grace in the procedure." Grace and doom coexist in her as historical inheritances, and as we observe her throughout the novel we are preparing to recognize what will happen in the end: the fulfillment of her grace, the accuracy of her restored character as an illustration of the selfish morality of her social class, is identical with her doom. " 'I'm well again,'" she tells Tommy Barban. "'And being well perhaps I've gone back to my true self—I suppose my grandfather was a crook and I'm a crook by heritage.'" (Earlier we had learned that her rich grandfather had begun his career as a horse thief.) Nicole's surrender to Tommy is given an even wider range of historical connotation in the following passage: "Moment by moment all that Dick taught her fell away and she was ever nearer to what she had been in the beginning, prototype of that obscure yielding up of swords that was going on in the world about her. Tangled with love in the moonlight she welcomed the anarchy of her lover."

Nicole's fulfillment, which is a journey back to her true nature, occurs in time, "moment by moment." It is historical in the personal sense of her individual development in the novel, and also in a larger sense that the novel forces upon us: the transfer of her allegiance, her money, and the power it represents, to a new force typified by a counterrevolutionary mercenary turned stockbroker. Nicole's yielding to Barban becomes an emblem of the yielding of order to disorder, as the crumbling actions of Book Three make clear. The outlaw lovers come together as each other's present opportunity for personal and social survival. In the final scene on the Riviera, Nicole "got to her knees" in a momentary and automatic response to Dick's "papal cross" over the beach that was once his "bright tan prayer rug"; when Tommy pulls "her firmly down," he exercises the discipline she requires to complete her liberation from Dick, and thus certifies the social character of her new self.

Dick's mock blessing of the beach is also a certification of his own freedom from the illusions which have controlled his life. The papal image compels us, moreover, to reconsider the nature of Dick's situation. In his "General Plan" Fitzgerald had described his hero as a "spoiled priest." The term has more than a metaphoric rightness. In the only scene in which we see Dick as a doctor among patients, he tries to comfort an American woman artist whose life had become, incurably, "a living agonizing sore." She reproaches him for his "beautiful words" of comfort, and Dick can only stoop and kiss her forehead and say, as liturgy, " 'we must all try to be good.' " A psychiatrist *manqué,* he performs an essentially religious ritual. We are invited to imagine that in certain circumstances Dick Diver might very well have chosen a priestly vocation like his father's, and that in fact he does perform a priestly role. This is true of his actions not only as a doctor but as a husband and lover as well. To strive to create illusions of invulnerable beauty and goodness is much like presiding over a ritual. Dick's situation is defined by the intersection of two incompatible thrusts: the desire for a permanent "lush midsummer moment outside of time"—for the tender night of Keats's nightingale—and the corrosive action of time and history, "the weariness, the fever, and the fret." Deprived of illusion by time and by new social realities evolving within it, Dick is reduced to sitting in his chair "listening to the buzz of the electric clock, listening to time."

This last image arrives with such powerful effect because it locates the heart of Dick's problem. As a "spoiled priest," as a lover and hero, Dick wants to occupy time entirely, to fill it so completely with his being that it ceases to matter. In his student days, Zurich had been for him "the centre of the great Swiss watch," a sanctuary where time is still. To be at the centre of the watch is to be at Eliot's still point "outside of time." The opposite of this condition is to be totally aware of time, to hear it as a pure substance. Terms like "waste" and "lost" and "spent," applied throughout the book to time, indicate a frame of mind which interprets time as a usable substance, a commodity like money. Both time and money are infinitely calculable to the calculating mind. For Nicole, "the years slipped away by clock and calender and birthday." Time is the reservoir of her power, and as it slips away she learns more and more the need to *use* it: " 'I've lost so much time.' " But for Dick, "time stood still and then every few years accelerated in a rush, like a quick rewind of a film."

It is clear that Dick feels most alive when "time stood still." He feels increasingly powerless when time accelerates, as it does in Book Three. But it is a mistake to see Dick as entirely passive in this book. Faced with the collapse of his marriage, his career, and his friendships, Dick needs an action through which to extricate himself with some degree of dignity. In an important conversation with Rosemary, shortly before the Cannes episode, Dick provides the reader with a clue to his behavior in Book Three. He lectures Rosemary on the dangers to the success of a dramatic illusion when an actress responds normally to certain extreme events on stage. Her aim should be to get the audience's attention away from the event and back to herself, that is, to the role she is performing. To accomplish this she must sometimes " 'do something unexpected.' " " 'If the audience thinks the character is hard,' " for example, " 'she goes soft on them—if they think she's soft she goes hard.' " " 'The unexpected thing,' " Dick explains, maneuvers " 'the audience back from the objective fact to yourself. *Then* you slide into character again.' "

The comments apply entirely to his own situation. The publicly deteriorating circumstances of his life are the "events" which distract attention from his dramatic "role" or character. He is an actor losing his audience, and his desperate need, for dignity and for a coherent identity, is to recapture enough attention to the self-created illusion of himself to permit an orderly and fairly decent exit. From this point of view—supported by Fitzgerald's comment that Dick's intention dominated the final section of the novel—his departure is a deliberate choice, an acceptance of necessities generated by earlier choices. In effect Dick arranges for his own demise, thus preserving his superiority over the Warrens and Tommy Barban. As he fades deeper into the American provincial landscape in the moving final paragraph, we sense that something of value, self-deceptive and vulnerable as it is, fades with him. His disappearance might be taken as a "plaintive anthem," if the novel's title is indeed meant to remind us of the "deceiving" illusions of Keats's nightingale.

In any case it is certain that throughout the novel the reader has witnessed and participated in a struggle between illusion and reality, a struggle contained within the ambiguities of character and episode. The major version of the conflict is the "intensely calculated" life of the Divers, an unstable union of Dick's manners and traditional virtues and Nicole's wealth. There is indeed an "incalculable element," which is how Dick first appears to the book's arch calculator, Baby Warren. His services can be counted up and purchased, but the inner expenses cannot be translated into cash. In the final phases of Dick's decline, as he more and more just sits and listens, unable to imagine a future, we learn that an "incalculable story was telling itself inside him." This is the real story of the novel: the human costs of the bargain with unstable illusions. The unspoken story represents a countermovement to the events, a journey back to beginnings in the American landscape—or, to use another of the cinematic images from the text—a "rewind," consummated in the fade-out of the final paragraph.

Tender Is the Night submits American myths to the test of time. The conflict is enacted by the reader as he experiences the world of the fiction in the process of change. Historical awareness is, as it were, a product of the book. Fitzgerald's understanding of change and of the social structure of feeling had advanced considerably since *The Great Gatsby*. The earlier novel had tried to grasp the world more or less mythically; *Tender Is the Night* creates, with the reader's collaboration, a perspective unrelentingly historical. The reader's work is to assemble the materials of the novel into a fictive history which, once attained, is surely one of the most remarkably illuminating experiences in American literature.

THE PROGRAM, SEPTEMBER 5 THROUGH

SEPTEMBER 8, 1967

Conferences

I. DICKENS

Directed by Gordon N. Ray, John Simon Guggenheim Memorial Foundation

1. Recent Dickensian Studies
   Edgar Johnson, City College, New York
2. Dickens's Later Novels: Their Shadows and Realities
   K. J. Fielding, University of Edinburgh
3. Dickens and the Comedy of Humors
   Northrop Frye, Victoria College, University of Toronto

II. CRITICISM IN RENEWAL: THE NOVEL

Directed by Roy Harvey Pearce, University of California (San Diego)

1. Form and Meaning in Nineteenth-Century Fiction
   J. Hillis Miller, The Johns Hopkins University
2. The Author and His Readers: Meditations on a Stendhalian Metaphor
   Stephen Gilman, Harvard University
3. The Person of the Maker
   George P. Elliott, Syracuse University

III. ORAL TRADITION AND LITERARY FORM

Directed by Albert B. Friedman, Claremont Graduate School

1. The Traditional Singer as Artist
   Robert P. Creed, State University of New York (Stony Brook)
2. Aesthetic Form in British and American Folk Narrative
   Richard M. Dorson, Indiana University
3. Musical Tunes and Recited Verses
   Bertrand H. Bronson, University of California (Berkeley)

IV. PRIZE ESSAYS

1. The Norm of Character in the English Gothic Novel
   Francis Russell Hart, University of Virginia
2. Jenny Wren
   Mrs. Toby A. Olshin, University of Pennsylvania
3. The Journey Back: *Tender Is the Night* and Forms of History in the American Novel
   Alan Trachtenberg, The Pennsylvania State University

Honorable Mention

Moll Flanders and the Problem of the Novel as Literary Art
Peter Elbow, Brandeis University

Gutenberg and the Graces: A Study of the Effect of Literacy on Poetic Form
Norman Austin, University of California (Los Angeles)

Ruth M. Adams, Wellesley College; Gellert S. Alleman, Rutgers University, Newark; Marcia Allentuck, City College, New York; Valborg Anderson, Brooklyn College; Sister Ann Edward, Chestnut Hill College; L. M. Antalis, Ohio University, Belmont County; Mother Mary Anthony, Rosemont College; Stanford Apseloff, Kent State University; Richard Arthur, Rutgers University; Norman Austin, University of California, Los Angeles; Melvin Backman, Clarkson College; Nancy Bailey, University of Guelph; Ashur Baizer, Ithaca College; Sheridan Baker, University of Michigan; C. L. Barber, Indiana University; Louise K. Barnett, York Junior College; Rev. J. Robert Barth, s.j., Canisius College; Phyllis Bartlett, Queens College; Elaine Hoffman Baruch, York College; Jerome Beaty, Emory University; L. A. Beaurline, University of Virginia; Rev. John E. Becker, s.j., Yale University; Alice R. Bensen, Eastern Michigan University; Bernard Benstock, Kent State University; Sister Bernarda Jaques, c. s. j., The College of St. Rose; Henry A. Blackwell, St. Xavier College; Rev. Vincent F. Blehl, s.j., Fordham University; Charles R. Blyth, Jr., Brandeis University; Anne C. Bolgan, University of Western Ontario; Sister M. Bonaventure, Nazareth College of Rochester; Brother Francis Bowers, f.s.c., Manhattan College; Rev. John D. Boyd, s.j., Fordham University; Frank Brady, Pennsylvania State University; Bertrand H. Bronson, University of California, Berkeley; Margaret M. Bryant, Brooklyn College; Jean R. Buchert, University of North Carolina, Greensboro; Brother Daniel Burke, f.s.c., La Salle College; Robert B. Burlin, Bryn Mawr College; Douglas Bush, Harvard University; Mervin Butovsky, Sir George Williams University; Robert Buttel, Temple University; Joseph L. Cady, Jr., Columbia University; Grace J. Calder, Hunter College; John Cameron, Amherst College; Ronald Campbell, Harcourt, Brace & World, Inc.; James Van Dyck Card, Old Dominion College; Eric W. Carlson, University of Connecticut; G. H. Carrithers, Jr., State University of New York, Buffalo; Joan P. Caton, George Washington University; Sister Mary Charles, Immaculata College; Hugh C. G. Chase, Bristol, N.H.; Howell D. Chickering, Jr., Amherst College; Kent Christensen, Upsala College; John A. Christie, Vassar College; Judith P. Clark, Lindenwood College; Mother Mary Clement, s.h.c.j., Holy Child Academy, Rosemont College; James L. Clifford, Columbia University; James H. Coberly, George Washington University; Arthur N. Collins, State University of New York, Albany; Rowland L. Collins, University of Rochester; David Cowden, Swarthmore College; James M. Cox, Dartmouth College; Robert P. Creed, State University of New York, Stony Brook; J. V. Cunningham, Brandeis University; Rev. John V. Curry, s.j., Loyola Seminary; Curtis Dahl, Wheaton College; Charles

R. Dahlberg, Queens College; Lloyd J. Davidson, Virginia Military Institute; Gwenn Davis, Bryn Mawr College; Winifred M. Davis, Hunter College; Robert Adams Day, Queens College; Thomas Deegan, St. Xavier College; Mary E. Dichmann, University of Southwestern Louisiana; E. Talbot Donaldson, Columbia University; John H. Dorenkamp, Holy Cross College; Richard M. Dorson, Indiana University; Marjorie Downing, Scripps College; Esther M. Doyle, Juniata College; Victor Doyno, State University of New York, Buffalo; Barbara J. Dunham, George Washington University; Thomas F. Dunn, Canisius College; David A. Dushkin, Random House, Inc.; Benjamin W. Early, Mary Washington College, University of Virginia; Edward R. Easton, Pace College; Irvin Ehrenpreis, University of Virginia; George P. Elliott, Syracuse University; Mrs. George P. Elliott, Syracuse, N.Y.; Richard Ellmann, Northwestern University; William R. Elton, University of California, Riverside; Martha Winburn England, Queens College; David V. Erdman, New York Public Library; Sister Marie Eugenie, Immaculata College; Doris V. Falk, Douglass College, Rutgers University; H. Alfred Farrell, Lincoln University; George S. Fayen, Yale University; N. N. Feltes, Emory University; Sidney Feshbach, State University of New York, Stony Brook; K. J. Fielding, Edinburgh University; Edward Fiess, State University of New York, Stony Brook; John J. Filor, Canisius College; John J. Fisher, Jr., Goshen College; Mary O. Fisher, University of Illinois, Chicago Circle; P. D. Fleck, University of Western Ontario; Edward G. Fletcher, University of Texas; George H. Ford, University of Rochester; Robert D. Foulke, Trinity College; Robert C. Fox, St. Francis College; Joseph I. Fradin, State University of New York, Buffalo; Richard L. Francis, Brown University; Barbara Friedberg, Columbia University; Albert B. Friedman, Claremont Graduate School; Northrop Frye, Victoria College, University of Toronto; C. E. Fullman, Upsala College; Paul Fussell, Jr., Rutgers University; George Rhys Garnett, University of British Columbia; Harry R. Garvin, Bucknell University; Alexander Gelley, Cornell University; Mary E. Giffin, Vassar College; Stephen Gilman, Harvard University; Anthony Gosse, Bucknell University; Matthew Grace, City College, New York; Thomas J. Grace, Fairfield University; James Gray, Bishop's University; Rose B. Green, Cabrini College; James J. Greene, City College, New York; Allen Guttmann, Amherst College; Gordon S. Haight, Yale University; Judith A. Hakola, University of Maine; Robert Halsband, Columbia University; Victor M. Hamm, Marquette University; James R. Harmon, Charles Scribner's Sons; Richard Harrier, New York University; Mason Harris, Simon Fraser University; Francis Russell Hart, University of Virginia; John A. Hart, Carnegie Institute of Technology; Carol A. Hawkes, Finch College; Ann L. Hayes, Carnegie Institute of Technology; David Hayman, University of Iowa; Peter Heidtmann, Ohio University; Rolanne Henry, Rutgers University, Newark; Mrs. Charles G. Hill, Queens College; Rev. William Bernard Hill, s.j., Loyola Seminary; Stanley M. Holberg, St. Lawrence University; Laurence B. Holland, Princeton University; Norman N. Holland, State University of New York, Buffalo; Frank S. Hook, Lehigh University; Andrew G. Hoover, Oberlin College; Vivian C. Hopkins, State University of New York, Albany; Harry R. Hoppe, Michigan State University; Donald R. Howard, The Johns Hopkins University; John F. Hulcoop, University of British Columbia; J. Paul Hunter, Emory University; Eleanor N. Hutchens, University of Alabama, Huntsville; Samuel Hynes, Swarthmore College; Julia H. Hysham, Skidmore College; Edward D. Ives, University of Maine; Sears Jayne, Queens College; Edgar Johnson, City College, New York; George W. Johnson, Temple University; S. F. Johnson, Columbia University; Leah E. Jordan, West Chester State College; Marjorie R. Kaufman, Mount Holyoke College; John E. Keating, Kent State University; Frederick M. Keener, Columbia University; Robert Kellogg, University of Virginia; Walter B. Kelly, Mary Washington College, University of Virginia; Sister Eileen Campion Kennedy, College of St. Elizabeth; James G. Kennedy, Upsala College; Veronica M. S. Kennedy, St. John's University; George Kent, Quinnipiac College; Earl A. Knies, Ohio University; Kathrine Koller, University of Rochester; Joaquin C. Kuhn, Stillman College; Eric W. Kurtz, Wellesley College; Lincoln F. Ladd, University of North Carolina, Greensboro; Parker B. Ladd, Charles Scribner's Sons; Rev. John P. Lahey, s.j., Le Moyne College; John Lauber, University of Alberta; Rev. Henry St. C. Lavin, s.j., University of Scranton; Lewis Leary, Columbia University; Francis Noel Lees, University of Manchester; Seymour Levitan, University of British Columbia; Christiaan T. Lievestro, Drexel Institute of Technology; Dwight N. Lindley, Hamilton College; Jean S. Lindsay, Hunter College; George de F. Lord, Yale University; Joseph Lovering, Canisius College; Fei-Pai Lu, C. W. Post College, Long Island University; Sister Mary Aloyse Lubin, College of St. Elizabeth; Mary Elizabeth MacAndrew, Columbia University; Isabel G. MacCaffrey, Bryn Mawr College; Patrick J. McCarthy, University of California, Santa Barbara; Muriel McClanahan, George Washington University; Frederick P. W. McDowell, University of Iowa; Manfred Mackenzie, University of Adelaide; Richard A. Macksey, The Johns Hopkins University; Lorna E. MacLean, Sir George Williams University; Robert Simpson McLean, Queensborough Community College; Mother C. E. Maguire, Newton College of the Sacred Heart; Daniel Majdiak, University of Illinois; Louis Martz, Yale University; Jackson Mathews, Bollingen Foundation; John Kelly Mathison, University of Wyoming; B. H. Mayne, University of British Columbia; Robert D. Mayo, Northwestern University; Donald C. Mell, Jr., Middlebury College; John H. Middendorf, Columbia University; J. Hillis Miller, The Johns Hopkins University; Milton Millhauser, University of Bridgeport; Mother Grace Monahan, o.s.u., College of New Rochelle; John N. Morrel, Rutgers University; George L. Nesbitt, Hamilton College; Francis X. Newman, The Johns Hopkins University; Helaine Newstead, Hunter College; Bink Noll, Beloit College; Rev. William T. Noon, s.j., Le Moyne College; Sister M. Norma, Albertus Magnus College; Paul E. O'Connell, Prentice-Hall, Inc.; Mrs. Toby Olshin, Philadelphia; Rev. Joseph E. O'Neill, s.j., Fordham University; Tucker Orbison, Bucknell University; Mother Thomas Aquinas O'Reilly, o.s.u., College of New Rochelle; James M. Osborn, Yale University; Bernard Ostendorf, Albert Ludwig University, Freiburg; Alicia Ostriker, Rutgers University; Charles A. Owen, Jr., University of Connecticut; Stephen C. Paine, Bradley University; Robert B. Partlow, Jr., Southern Illinois University; Sister Catherine Mary Patten, Marymount Manhattan College; Robert L. Patten, Bryn Mawr College; Roy

Harvey Pearce, University of California, San Diego; Norman Holmes Pearson, Yale University; Harry William Pedicord, Thiel College; Candido Perez Gallego, Madrid University; Marjorie Perloff, Catholic University of America; Carl A. Peterson, Oberlin College; Henry H. Peyton III, Memphis State University; Frederick Plotkin, State University of New York, Buffalo; Robert O. Preyer, Brandeis University; Jonathan R. Price, Yale University; Martin Price, Yale University; Max Putzel, University of Connecticut; Richard E. Quaintance, Jr., Douglass College, Rutgers University; Virginia L. Radley, Russell Sage College; Helen Randall, Smith College; Isabel E. Rathborne, Hunter College; Gordon N. Ray, Guggenheim Foundation; Donald H. Reiman, The Carl H. Pforzheimer Library; Joseph N. Riddel, State University of New York, Buffalo; Sister Rita Margaret, Caldwell College; Carmen L. Rivera, Mary Washington College, University of Virginia; Gertrude B. Rivers, Howard University; Leo Rockas, Briarcliff College; Francis X. Roellinger, Oberlin College; William John Roscelli, University of Florida; Sister Rose Bernard Donna, c.s.j., The College of St. Rose; Michael Rosenblum, Indiana University; Claire Rosenfield, Radcliffe Institute; Irene Samuel, Hunter College; B. N. Schilling, University of Rochester; Helene B. M. Schnabel, New York; Robert Scholes, University of Iowa; Flora Rheta Schreiber, John Jay College of Criminal Justice; H. T. Schultz, Dartmouth College; Joseph Sendry, Catholic University of America; Susan Field Senneff, Columbia University; Richard Sexton, Fordham University; Gordon M. Shedd, Pennsylvania State University; G. David Sheps, Sir George Williams University; James D. Simmonds, University of Pittsburgh; Calvin Skaggs, Drew University; Joseph Evans Slate, University of Texas; Carol H. Smith, Douglass College, Rutgers University; Nolan E. Smith, Yale University; Nelle Smither, Douglass College, Rutgers University; George Soule, Carleton College; Ian Sowton, University of Alberta; J. Gordon Spaulding, University of British Columbia; Mark Spilka, Brown University; H. D. Sproule, Dalhousie University; Nathan C. Starr, New School for Social Research; Sarah Susan Staves, University of Virginia; C. N. Stavron, Canisius College; Oliver Steele, University of Iowa; Lionel Stevenson, Duke University; Philip Stevick, Temple University; Vincent Stewart, Virginia Polytechnic Institute; Fred. E. Stockholder, University of British Columbia; Donald R. Stoddard, Skidmore College; Jean Sudrann, Mount Holyoke College; Maureen T. Sullivan, University of Pennsylvania; Joseph H. Summers, Michigan State University; Donald R. Swanson, Upsala College; Anne Robb Taylor, Skidmore College; Ruth Z. Temple, Brooklyn College; Sister Mary Teresita Fay, Marymount Manhattan College; Charles B. Teske, Oberlin College; Henry F. Thoma, Houghton Mifflin Co.; Wright Thomas, New York State University College, Cortland; R. J. Thompson, Canisius College; Stanley Tick, San Francisco State College; Michael Timko, Queens College; Nancy M. Tischler, Pennsylvania State University; Robert Tisdale, Carleton College; R. C. Townsend, Amherst College; Alan Trachtenberg, Pennsylvania State University; Donald Tritschler, Skidmore College; Margret G. Trotter, Agnes Scott College; Mary Curtis Tucker, Marietta, Ga.; S. O. A. Ullmann, Union College; Helen M. Ulrich, Queens College; John Unterecker, Columbia University; Helen H. Vendler,

Boston University; David M. Vieth, Southern Illinois University; Sister M. Vincentia, o.p., Albertus Magnus College; Sister M. Vivien, Caldwell College; Sister Mary Julius Wagner, s.c., College of St. Elizabeth; Eugene M. Waith, Yale University; Andrew J. Walker, Georgia Institute of Technology; M. Elizabeth Waterston, Wellington College, University of Guelph; Charlotte C. Watkins, Howard University; Thomas L. Watson, Louisiana State University; Herbert Weisinger, State University of New York, Stony Brook; Mother E. White, Newton College of the Sacred Heart; Rev. Joseph Wiesenfarth, f.s.c., Manhattan College; Alan Wilde, Temple University; Elizabeth Wiley, Susquehanna University; Maurita Willett, University of Illinois, Chicago Circle; Lyle Givens Williams, University of Southwestern Louisiana; Marilyn L. Williamson, Oakland University, Dorothy M. Willis, New Haven, Conn.; Edwin G. Wilson, Wake Forest College; W. K. Wimsatt, Yale University; Calhoun Winton, University of South Carolina; Philip Withim, Bucknell University; Patricia A. Wolfe, Douglass College, Rutgers University; R. G. Woodman, University of Western Ontario; Carl Woodring, Columbia University; Sister Mary Xavier, Chestnut Hill College; William H. Youngren, Smith College.